HISTORY snapshots™

Europe, Ancient and Classical

hexco
©2020 Hexco Academic

The average history textbook is a wealth of information but often includes almost too much for quick study - leaving students to sieve through lines of text to understand the foundation of the issue at hand. The goal of our *Snapshots* series is to give students key information in bite-sized and manageable pieces without losing the trivia element that makes history fun.

Disclaimer notice: The content of any history contest is not limited to the events in this book. Dates and facts have been verified by at least two reliable sources, however, we encourage you to contact us if any information contained in this book is historically inaccurate.

Printed in the United States of America
ISBN-13: 978-1-56323-000-4

First printing, 2020
Hexco Academic
P.O. Box 199
Hunt, TX 78024
www.hexco.com

Author - Michael R. Cude, PhD, Schreiner University
Editors - Keisha Bedwell, Jennifer King, Beth Mader, Noel Putnam, Linda Tarrant
Internal Design and Cover - Nicole Huff

ORDERING INFORMATION
Special discounts are available on quantity purchases by schools, teams, corporations, associations, etc. For details, contact the publisher at the address above. Bookstores and wholesalers interested in resale options for this publication or *History Essentials* are encouraged to contact Hexco at (800) 391-2891 or email hexco@hexco.com.

DEDICATION

This book is dedicated to Simona Cude and Ian Cude
for their ongoing support.

TABLE OF CONTENTS

INTRODUCTION

Europe - While this term is normal today, the precise start of its use as a geographical marker are unknown. Conventional use of the term started with the Greeks. According to Greek stories, Europa was an ancient Phoenician princess abducted by the god **Zeus**. She bore his children, one of whom was King **Minos** of Crete. Greek scholars began using the term as a geographical marker by the sixth and fifth centuries BCE, dividing their known world into three parts: Europe, Asia, and Libya (North Africa). They categorized Europe as the lands north of the Mediterranean and west of the Don River in what is now Russia. The idea of being "European" did not develop until the Carolingian Renaissance in the ninth century CE.

Where is Europe? - In the most expansive definition, Europe spreads roughly east to west from the Ural Mountains in Russia to Iceland and north to south from Arctic Scandinavia to the Mediterranean. The precise borders, both geographically and culturally, will depend upon whom you ask, as illustrated by debates over whether Turkey should join the present-day European Union. Many people divide Europe culturally between Eastern, Western, and Central Europe, as well as between Northern and Southern Europe. Where to draw these regional boundaries is, again, contested. While it is customary to identify Europe as one of the seven continents, some identify it as part of a broader continent of Eurasia, given its lack of geographical separation.

Western Civilization - This term is a modern attempt to define a common, unique European culture and intellectual tradition rooted in **Greco-Roman** and **Judeo-Christian** traditions. The term also accounts for peoples and cultures of European descent outside of the Europe proper. Debates exist over how to define this term. To what extent should we consider ancient cultures beyond the Greeks and Romans within this framework? How do we account for the influence of non-European cultures and ideas on European civilization? Historically, the centers of Western civilization were in the Eastern Mediterranean but gradually shifted more northward and westward. Ancient and classical Western civilization was heavily influenced by Near Eastern culture, and it was not until the early modern period that a clear sense of separation from the **Near East** began to develop.

CHAPTER 1

Prehistory and the Beginnings of Civilization

THE STONE AGE

Prehistory

History as a discipline is based predominantly upon our accounting of the past using written records. This contrasts with fields such as **archaeology** and **paleontology** which are focused more on non-written artifacts. The term "prehistory" refers to the periods of life on earth before the development of writing by humans in the 3000s BCE.

The Stone Age

This is the period when human beings utilized stones as their primary source of toolmaking. The terms **"Paleolithic," "Mesolithic," "Neolithic**" mean "Old Stone Age," "Middle Stone Age," and "New Stone Age," respectively. The Paleolithic period began with the development of the first stone tools roughly three million years ago, lasting to 20,000 years ago. The Neolithic period lasted until roughly 8,000 years ago. This period saw a shift toward settled lifestyles and more complex toolmaking as animal life changed due to the end of the Ice Age. The Neolithic period lasted until the start of the Bronze Age around 3000 BCE. It marks the transition to agricultural civilizations.

Why Humans?

Humans thrived for a variety of reasons. They benefited from being **hominids**, which allowed them to travel great distances and utilize their hands while moving. Opposable thumbs allowed them to manipulate their environment to survive. A diversity of diet allowed early humans to adjust to different ecosystems and have a relatively stable food supply. Humans then

*The oldest known human fossil remains were discovered in present-day Ethiopia in the **East African Rift Valley** and dated to around 160,000 years ago. It is also the site of older hominid remains. The **Horn of Africa** is commonly accepted as the starting point of humanity.*

excelled due to advanced cognitive skills, learning through problem solving, memorization, and sharing information through language. The harnessing of fire allowed the expansion of human diets, with safer, cooked food. Fire was also a source of protection and granted the ability to live in colder climates. More stable nutrition allowed greater population growth and healthier physical development, essential for brainpower.

First Migrations to Europe

Modern man likely originated in Africa, spreading across the globe as the climate became warmer due to a shift in the Earth's rotation. The end of the last **Ice Age**, which concluded around 10,000 BCE, made human migrations easier, with more temperate climates and landmasses becoming more accessible. This development allowed modern humans (*homo sapiens*) to enter Europe around 40,000 years ago. While they arrived following big game herds, this era marked the final phase of prehistoric migrations.

Neanderthals

Humans were preceded into Europe by other early humanoids that no longer exist, such as the Neanderthals who arrived in Europe around 300,000 years ago. Neanderthals were shorter, stockier, and stronger than humans. They survived chiefly by hunting large animals, notably bison. Although there is debate over their exact level of intelligence compared to humans, they appear to have had elements of culture, such as language and artwork. Whether the Neanderthals' disappearance was caused by the arrival of humans or by other means, such as natural disasters, is debated. Evidence suggests that they intermixed with humans, either through peaceful integration or by conquest. Traces of Neanderthal DNA remain in modern people of European ancestry.

The exact point when humans discovered how to control fire is unknown, but by 150,000 years ago it was widely used for hunting, cooking, and toolmaking.

Neanderthals

Prehistoric Lifestyles

Early humans lived as **hunter-gatherers** by hunting animals, such as mastodons, deer, bison, and reindeer, and also by foraging fruits, berries, roots, seeds, nuts, and wild grains. The need to cover wide distances to produce food encouraged smaller bands of 20-30 people and caused constant migration and dispersion. Interaction with other humans led to competition and conflict but also to cooperation and trade. Prehistoric humans utilized stone tools for hammering, cutting, and carving. By their arrival in Europe, early humans were fabricating non-stone tools, such as spears and baskets. They had also established artwork, music, clothing, and jewelry. **Prehistoric cave paintings** in France and Spain from around 30,000 BCE depict game animals, as do small sculptures made of stone or bone. Depictions of fire dances and funerary remains show early forms of culture and religion.

Stone Tool

*The **Chauvet Cave** in southern France includes some of the best-preserved prehistoric cave paintings in Europe, depicting hundreds of animals of different species, including horses, rhinoceroses, and bison.*

The First Agricultural Revolution

A big leap for human culture came around 10,000 BCE with the **Neolithic Revolution**, which started in the Near East and lasted 5,000 years. This period started the widespread domestication of plants and animals for human consumption. Warming climates drove this process. The end of the Ice Age caused the extinction of many big game animals, while also facilitating new plant growth. Full-time farmers and pastoralists became common. Agriculture spread to Europe from here. Wheat and barley were developed as the **staple crops** after being cultivated as wild plants, followed by many other fruit and vegetable products. Animal domestication followed. Sheep, goats, cattle, and pigs were all developed in the Near East during this time.

Sedentary Lifestyles

With more geographically fixed production, humans moved toward settlement rather than nomadic lifestyles. Agriculture increased the control and expansion of the food supply, allowing more stable populations. Large numbers of children were a burden in hunter-gatherer societies, causing harder travel and creating more mouths to feed, but they became an asset in agricultural communities. Agricultural societies had more food to support children and benefited from an increased labor supply. By 3000 BCE, most of Europe had shifted to sedentary lifestyles.

Nomadic Pastoralism

Nomadic culture did not completely disappear but rather took a new form. Nomadic and semi-nomadic pastoralism developed with the domestication of herd animals, such as sheep and cattle. This lifestyle saw peoples migrate with domesticated herds between viable grazing areas. Accordingly, horse domestication began in Central Asia during the Neolithic Revolution and

*Prehistoric hunters targeted large **megafauna**, which are now extinct, such as mastodons, giant bison, and giant elk. Giant bulls called **aurochs** hunted in the late stone age likely became the source of domesticated cattle.*

arrived in Europe by 3000 BCE. Horses were originally hunted for food and supplementary items, such as leather. Once domesticated, they became the most valuable animal as a beast of burden for agriculture, long-distance travel, and military uses.

The Fertile Crescent

The region commonly known today as the Middle East, Near East, or Southwest Asia, the Fertile Crescent was the starting location of the Neolithic Revolution. The exact starting point and process of the Neolithic Revolution is unknown, although the oldest evidence of settled agriculture exists at **Tell Aswad**, near Damascus, Syria. Sites such as **Gesher** in Israel and **Göbekli Tepe** in Turkey suggest that people living as hunter-gatherers, and still lacking advanced pottery and metals, established the first settlements. Agriculture followed settlement, not the other way around.

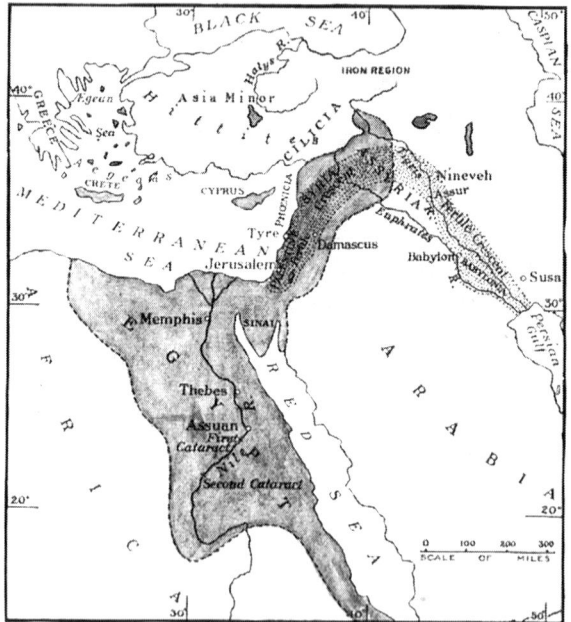

Fertile Crescent

The First Civilizations

A civilization in the context of ancient history refers to a larger-scale society with a complex social organization based around both rural and urban lifestyles. The first large-scale civilizations developed around 5000 BCE in the Near East following the Neolithic Revolution. They were located on **river**

The discovery at Göbekli Tepe appears to be a temple and includes many stone pillars up to 10 feet tall with animal carvings on them. It is unclear how they were produced or how they were used for ceremonies as they are dated to before the development of metallurgy.

basins, due to access to a water supply and rich soil deposits. Agricultural settlement saw the development of new tools. Clay pottery and woven baskets stored food and were used to create more complex meals. Irrigation and aqueducts moved water to farmlands and cities and controlled flooding. New manufacturing tools allowed new trades, such as carpentry and masonry, for more stable homesteads of wood, clay, and stone.

Food Surplus and Urbanization

The critical step for a society was to reach a **food surplus**, producing more food than needed for community sustenance. This surplus allowed people to pursue jobs outside of farming. They became skilled craftsmen, inventors, scholars, soldiers, religious leaders, or many other occupations that benefited the community. Towns and cities grew in population as the primary domain of non-agricultural workers, producing manufactured goods, cultural products, and political leaders in a symbiotic relationship with the countryside.

Specialization

This career specialization allowed a more rapid growth in economic production, intellectual life, and culture. A farmer, for example, would produce food eaten by a scholar, who built knowledge about the world that led to the invention of a new tool or better management of growing. This period saw societies start to learn about the seasons and develop early concepts of time. This knowledge helped management of growing seasons and set the stage for the first science and mathematics.

Early Religions

Specialization, likewise, allowed the development of codified religions with official priestly classes. These early religions were predominantly **polytheistic**, and the gods represented different natural phenomena or creatures.

Early Government

Civilization also saw the development of the first codified political leadership and laws to provide oversight of increasingly complex societies. These early leaders likely arose as military commanders who gained respect in their communities and utilized their authority to assert control over resources. They later utilized culture and religion to justify continued authority of their family lineage.

Civilizational Transfer to Europe

Civilizational developments transferred from the Near East into Europe via trade and migration, with the first farmers migrating into the continent around 6000 BCE from Anatolia. **Varna**, in present-day Bulgaria, has a burial site from around 5000 BCE and contains the oldest signs of civilization, including gold treasure and artwork suggesting a political hierarchy. Sites from around the same period show advanced learning of the natural world. Such a site is **Goseck's Circle** in Germany, which is a Stone Age solar calendar to measure solstices. By 3500 BCE, early civilizations had been established in Europe although most people still lived in the countryside.

Natural Heritage Site in Varna, Bulgaria

THE BRONZE AGE

Beginning Use of Bronze

The central new discovery after the Neolithic Revolution was the melting of copper, the most desirable metal of the time due to its malleability. When mixed with tin, or other metals, it produced bronze, a sturdier metal useful for forging tools and weapons.

By around 3000 BCE, stone tools were almost entirely obsolete in settled societies, marking the start of what historians call the Bronze Age. More reliable tools, such as plows and rakes, made agriculture even more efficient, as did metal tools in other trades, such as carpentry.

Bronze Age Tools

Written Language

The Bronze Age was also essential for the development of writing. The oldest known language is **Sumerian** in **Mesopotamia**, developed in the 3000s BCE. Writing is critical for the maintaining and sharing of knowledge. The Bronze Age, accordingly, started the academic discipline of history through the creation of written documents which recorded events.

Near East Civilizations

The first larger-scale civilization occurred in the region of Mesopotamia, around the Tigris and Euphrates Rivers in what is now Iraq. Starting in the 3000s BCE, similar organizations followed shortly thereafter in **Egypt** and **Anatolia**. These peoples contributed to early civilization in Europe as people, goods, and knowledge spread into Europe from the region.

Sumerians

The first of these groups were the Sumerians. The Sumerians were important for technological developments, such as metalworking, the wheel, and textiles. Their religion had the first clear anthropomorphized gods, each representing natural phenomena. The Sumerians also had an early literature that doubled as a history and talked about a heroic past, notably the *Epic of Gilgamesh*. Their political organization took the model of a **city-state**, each represented by

*The **Epic of Gilgamesh** doubled as a history for the ancient Sumerians. It told the story of a great Sumerian king pursuing trials from the gods which occurred before a great flood that ended his line of hero kings. Several other peoples in Mesopotamia embraced it as their origin story, including the Akkadians and Babylonians.*

an individual god. The Sumerians had a political hierarchy based around kings, with lesser nobility underneath them as administrators, followed by soldiers and bureaucrats. The **Akkadians**, from Northern Mesopotamia, later conquered the Sumerians to unify the region under a single rule.

Babylonians

The Akkadians were followed by the Babylonians. The Babylonians established standards in astronomy and mathematics and standardized weights and

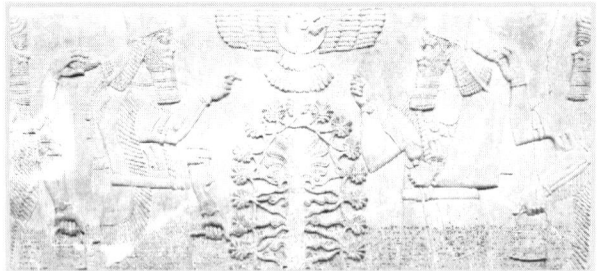

Ancient Sumerian Art

measures for economic exchanges. Their 60-based numeric system still influences present-day math in areas such as time and the measurement of circles. In addition, their **King Hammurabi** established the oldest known

King Hammurabi of Babylon established one of the oldest codified legal codes. It is known for its system of justice based on an "eye for an eye," meaning a punishment equal to the harm done by the crime. This punishment was not always a literal "eye," but it might mean a comparable monetary or physical punishment. Law was important for early civilization as it gave rulers legitimacy for bringing order and not just ruling as a strong man.

codified legal system. The **Hammurabi Code** outlined everything from property ownership, to social status, to criminal law. It legitimized the government as a source of order, beyond simply military power or religious legitimacy.

The Hittites

These Indo-European migrants established a kingdom in Anatolia (modern-day Turkey). A pastoralist culture, Hittites excelled with horses, invented the chariot, and served as political rivals to the other kingdoms in the Near East.

Ancient Egypt

Egypt was the most economically wealthy region, gifted by the consistent, manageable flooding of the **Nile River** and the fertile lands it produced. Egypt was also the longest lasting of the ancient kingdoms. Egypt became a primary trading partner with European cultures, particularly during the New Kingdom in the 1000s BCE, when its empire stretched into the **Levant**. Egypt also contributed much to cultural development, including early medical science, script writing using ink on **papyrus** (instead of burdensome stone carvings), and the precursor to our modern calendar. **Egyptian art** and architecture, such as columns, obelisks, and painted reliefs, extensively influenced the Greeks and Romans.

Ancient Egyptian Art

*As the longest lasting early civilization, historians divide Egyptian history into the three parts: the Old, the Middle, and the New Kingdom. These periods have clear distinctions. For example, the **pyramids** were built during the Old Kingdom. By the New Kingdom, pyramid building ceased, and Egyptian **pharaohs** were instead buried in necropoli in the **Valley of the Kings**.*

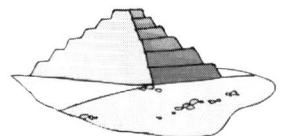

ANCIENT EUROPE

Changing Civilization

As civilization developed in the Near East, most Europeans still lived as hunter-gatherers. Some smaller agricultural communities pursued sustenance agriculture, with a few minor regional kingdoms controlling multiple villages. Most of these settlements had stone houses and built stone tombs and monuments, likely used for religious ceremonies that worshiped changes of the seasons and death. The development of metal tools in the Bronze Age was critical for Europe, because its soils were harder to cultivate. Bronze production normalized in the Aegean around 3000 BCE, but it was not standard through most of Europe until 2000 BCE.

Indo-European Migrations

A major change came to Europe due to the migration of Indo-European speaking peoples from Central Asia, starting around 3000 BCE. Originally herdsman, they came to dominate the region in large part due to their domestication of dairy cattle. The availability of the extra food source of beef and dairy gave them greater survival odds and larger population growth as they settled throughout Europe. The Indo-Europeans replaced preexisting cultural groups, whom they displaced or absorbed. The **Proto-Indo-Europeans** evolved into different groups across the continent and set the stage for classical European culture. The Greeks originated from Indo-European culture, as did the Romans, **Celts**, Germans, and many others.

Indo-European Language Group

This is a category of languages that originated from a Proto-Indo-European language and evolved into different modern languages. The geographical

*Basque is the only surviving pre-Indo-European language in present-day Europe. The other non-Indo-European languages, such as Finnish and Hungarian, part of the **Finno-Ugric language group**, arrived in Europe later.*

spread of the Indo-European culture was from India to Western Europe. Accordingly, almost every European language is from the Indo-European language group, which also includes Hindu and Persian.

Ancient European Society

By 2000 BCE, a common culture began to take shape in Europe, based on wheat as the staple crop and cattle for milk, labor, fertilizer, and meat. The use of wheeled vehicles and plows sped up agriculture, and civilization

Stonehenge, an Ancient Monument in England

saw the building of large stone monuments, such as Stonehenge. European societies came to revere great warriors, likely reflecting the pastoral nomadic culture brought by the Indo-Europeans. As a result, some of the best bronze weaponry arose in Europe. Europe was slow to imitate the nearby empires in political organization, remaining mostly rural and decentralized, but it did trade with them.

Ancient European Economy

Europe was a major source of precious metals, particularly copper, which its peoples traded to the large civilizations in the Near East for luxury goods. Trade allowed Europe to catch up, as it became part of a broader economic

Stonehenge was a stone solar calendar in England. It was used to measure solstices by marking the location of the sun throughout the year. Evidence of wooden versions (Woodhenge) suggests that these monuments served a funereal purpose, where wood monuments represented the world of the living and the stone monuments represented the world of the dead.

and cultural network throughout the Mediterranean region. Different regions specialized in certain products to maximize production and meet other needs in trade. This is called **trade specialization**.

Aegean Civilization

Accordingly, European civilization consolidated along the Mediterranean, using trade with the Near East to learn and develop. Urban centers developed in Southeastern Europe and Western Anatolia as trade hubs in the late 2000s BCE. These early cities included **Troy,** a fortified city in Western Anatolia, and **Knossos**, the oldest city in Europe which was located on the island of Crete. The location of islands, such as Crete and Cyprus, made them convenient stopping points for trade from Egypt and the Levant, which they used to build wealth. The islands in the Eastern Mediterranean (the Greek Isles) became linked by common culture and trade.

Minoans

The Minoans on Crete, named after King Minos of Knossos, were active in shipping across the Mediterranean by 1600 BCE. They began colonizing the other Greek Islands to establish mining operations, olive farming, and various manufacturing processes. Trade made Minoan elites very wealthy, with large palaces and many luxury goods. They built cities around massive palaces. Minoan leaders held political power using relatively large bureaucracies. They appear to have run on the city-state model and relied on trade to keep peace with each other and the larger empires in the Near East. They had no major fortresses but maintained a navy to protect trading vessels. The Minoans worshiped naturalist gods, but their religion was practiced in personal ceremonies with no large temples. Surviving texts appear to be economic records, but their language (**Linear A**) has yet to be translated.

Minoan cities were built around massive, maze-like palaces that likely served as the source of the myth of the labyrinth. These palaces had a large central throne room covered in fresco wall paintings and included early versions of windows and indoor plumbing.

Mycenaeans

The Minoans later received competition from the Mycenaeans, an Indo-European people that migrated into Greece from East-Central Europe starting around 1600 BCE. The Mycenaeans were a warrior society, utilizing chariots and advanced metalworking to conquer the region. Their warlords built large stone fortresses that established a centralized governance over the surrounding countryside. Their artwork mostly emphasized warfare. Once settled, they developed a large bureaucracy that oversaw agricultural production and manufacturing. Their religion included early versions of some Greek gods, such as Zeus, Poseidon, and Dionysus. They traded regularly with the Minoans and were influenced by them culturally. The Mycenaeans ultimately conquered the Minoans and eventually spread as far west as Italy. Linear A was replaced by the Mycenean language (**Linear B**).

Minoans and Myceneans in Greek culture

The Greeks likely evolved out of a merging of these two cultures. The Greeks later presented the Minoans as a domineering people who controlled the seas, demanding tribute. The stories of **Theseus** had the hero liberate Athens from the Minoans after he killed the **Minotaur,** while he was imprisoned by King Minos in the Labyrinth at Knossos. This story reflects the Minoan bull culture and their complex palace structures. The Greeks also showed the Minoans as technologically advanced, notably through the stories of **Daedalus**, a great inventor who designed their cities and the labyrinth. They presented the Myceneans as a warlike people founded by **Perseus**, who killed **Medusa**. The massive fortress at Mycenae was said to have been built by giants. Many Greek city-states claimed to have been founded by Myceneans.

*Minoan frescos illustrate that they revered bulls and had a sport of **bull-jumping**, a tradition that stills exists in parts of France and Spain.*

*The Cretan inventor **Daedalus** is known for the story of having developed wings of wax and feathers to escape imprisonment in Knossos. His son, **Icarus**, ignores his father's warnings of flying too close to the sun and dies when his wings melt.*

THE CLASSICAL NEAR EAST

The Iron Age

As civilization continued, technological advancements continued. A next important step came with the development of iron as the primary source of metallurgy. Iron was more prevalent than copper and tin but required higher temperatures to be smelted and separated from other elements. Once this technology developed, iron supplanted bronze in many areas, being stronger and more reliable, which started the Iron Age. Iron was used for better plows for tilling soil, and it was used to make weapons that were more lethal than the bronze counterparts. It could also be produced more cheaply. This process started around 1200 BCE and spread through Europe by 500 BCE.

Maritime Development

Another major technological leap in the Iron Age was maritime transportation, along with the development of cargo ships with larger, stronger hulls and better rigging and masts that could travel the open oceans with more substantial amounts of goods.

New Peoples and Empires in the Near East

The Iron Age saw the rise of new peoples that will influence European civilization, as well as the first Near Eastern empire.

The Sea People

A political reorganization of the Levant came about in part due to a mysterious group called the "Sea People," as identified by the Egyptians. Their origin is debated, but accounts suggest that they were a warrior

*Much of Western law and judicial practices have their roots in **Hebrew law**. Beyond the key principles outlined in the **Ten Commandments**, other standards, such as needing witnesses to a crime and a prohibition against self-incrimination, also have their roots there.*

people from Europe using iron weapons. They travelled around the Black Sea and the Eastern Mediterranean after 1200 BCE, invading and ravaging trade networks in the region. They helped put an end to the Hittite Kingdom and sacked the city of Troy. Those who attacked Egypt were crushed by **Ramses II**, but the destruction of trade networks saw a decline of New Kingdom Egypt.

Statue of Ramses II

Philistines

The Philistines, who may have been settled Sea People, become an example of a new state created out of the power vacuum in the Levant. They introduced olives and grapevines to the region, while becoming the main enemy of the ancient Hebrews, as identified in the story of **David and Goliath**.

Lydians

Another example were the Lydians who arose in Western Anatolia. With massive gold and silver deposits, they served as bankers for regional trade and perhaps invented coin money. Their legacy was represented by the Greeks in the story of King **Midas**, who could turn anything he touched into gold.

Phoenicians

Another important group were the Phoenicians, an offshoot of the Canaanites. The Phoenicians were based out of the island city of Tyre. They flourished economically as expert sailors and shipbuilders and established colonies across the Mediterranean. They were the first people to rely predominantly on sailing vessels, with oarsmen as backups, and

*The Greeks named their word for "book" after the main Phoenician port city exporting **papyrus**, a dried plant used like paper. This city was Byblos, which became the source of the word "Bible."*

25

	EGYPTIAN		SEMITIC	LATER EQUIVALENTS		
Values	Hieroglyphic	Hieratic	Phoenician	Greek	Roman	Hebrew
a	eagle			A	A	א 1
b	crane			B	B	ב 2
k (g)	throne			Γ	C	ג 3
ṭ (d)	hand			Δ	D	ד 4
h	mæander			E	E	ה 5
f	cerastes			Y	F	ו 6
z	duck			I	Z	ז 7
χ (kh)	sieve			H	H	ח 8
θ (th)	tongs			Θ	...	ט 9
i	parallels			I	I	י 10
k	bowl			K	K	כ 11
l	lioness			Λ	L	ל 12
m	owl			M	M	מ 13
n	water			N	N	נ 14
s	chairback			Ξ	X	ס 15
ā	......			O	O	ע 16
p	shutter			Π	P	פ 17
t' (ts)	snake			...	...	צ 18
q	angle			...	Q	ק 19
r	mouth			P	R	ר 20
š (sh)	inundated garden			Σ	S	ש 21
t	lasso			X +	T	ת 22
	I.	II.	III.	IV.	V. VI. VII.	

Ancient Language Chart

had an advanced navy. They traded timber, purple dye, and glassware that they produced, while otherwise acting as middlemen for Mediterranean trade. They were also important for creating the first alphabet, which linked defined symbols to phonetics in **Aramaic**, the common language of the Near East. The Phoenician alphabet was adopted by the Greeks and was the precursor to the modern-day Latin alphabet. The most powerful Phoenician kingdom became **Carthage** in modern-day Tunisia. Carthage was founded in 800 BCE and gained independence around 650 BCE when the Phoenician homeland was conquered by larger kingdoms.

Hebrews

The ancient Hebrews were the forebearers to the Israelites and Jews. According to their tradition, they were led by **Abraham** of Ur, whose descendants later formed a confederation of the 12 tribes of Israel. After entering Egypt, they fled persecution under the leadership of **Moses**. They settled in the southern Levant by the start of the Iron Age. Decentralized as a people, each tribe was led in battle by a "judge" who also provided legal

Passover is one of the three major Jewish pilgrimage holidays surviving from early Jewish history, honoring their escape from Egypt under the leadership of *Moses*. Its name referenced the passing over of Jewish homes in Egypt when God punished the Egyptians.

mediation. They unified under threat of extermination by the Philistines to establish their own kingdoms.

David and Solomon

David eventually unified the Israelites under a common kingdom around 1000 BCE. He established a new capital at Jerusalem to serve as the Jewish political and religious center, housing the **Ark of the Covenant** containing the original tablet with the Ten Commandments. Solomon built the kingdom into a regional power that saw much urban development. He also commissioned the building of the **First Temple**. After Solomon died, internal disputes caused the Hebrews to split into the two Kingdoms of Israel and Judah.

Captivity and Diaspora

Eventually, new empires conquered the Hebrews, starting with the **neo-Assyrians** in the 700s BCE, followed by the **neo-Babylonians**. The latter attempted to stamp out Jewish culture, destroying the Temple and forcibly relocating thousands to Babylon in what was called the Babylonian Captivity. The Jewish people became historical survivors and maintained their sense of independent identity and culture within these larger empires. They migrated across many parts of the Middle East, Africa, and Europe, creating a large **diaspora** of people living outside of their historical homeland.

Judaism

The consolidation of the Hebrews came due to their embracement of worship of a single God: **Yahweh**, meaning "the one who is." This turn to monotheism was the result of missionary efforts within the Hebrews to get their own people to reject the other gods worshipped in the region. This faith became Judaism. Judaism presented God as overseer of the universe, not defined exclusively by nature, who granted mankind oversight

*The **Ark of The Covenant** went missing after the destruction of the First Temple, and its current location is unknown. There are claims of people recovering the Ark, ranging from the Knights Templar to the Ethiopian Orthodox Church. There is no evidence that it is currently stored in a warehouse somewhere in the United States.*

of Earth. God provides the Hebrews guidelines for proper behavior in the Ten Commandments. Given to Moses by God, in addition to other laws and principles, they guide the organization of Jewish culture and society. These laws became a **covenant**, or contract, to which people will be held accountable. The faith eventually consolidated these rules and teachings in the **Torah**, the first five books in the Hebrew Bible. The Torah includes the history of the Jewish people and the teachings of its prophets. Judaism became the first monotheistic world religion.

The Persian Empire

Persepolis Ancient Ruins

The Persians, or Achaemenids, established the largest empire in the Near East up to this point. The Persians originated as a nomadic people from the **Iranian Plateau. Cyrus the Great** united them in a mission of conquest in the 500s BCE. At its peak, the Persian Empire spread from Central Asia to Egypt. Cyrus' successor, **Darius I**, ruled a multinational empire from their capital **Persepolis** and allowed local peoples to determine their own systems of administration. So long as everyone paid

The Hebrew traditions reflect stories and laws from earlier peoples in the Near East from which the Hebrews arose. For example, there are similarities between the Epic of Gilgamesh *and the story of* **Noah**. *The Hebrews were potentially part of the Canaanites before separating from them.*

tribute and swore loyalty, they were treated
as equals within the empire. For example,
Darius liberated the Hebrews from
Babylon and let them manage their former
territories. The empire also created a free-
trade zone within the empire and expanded
infrastructure to connect the different
regions. Persian culture and politics
influenced the direction of Europe in the
classical period through their interaction
with the Greeks.

Ancient Persian Art

Zoroastrianism

Zoroastrianism was the Persian religion named
after its founder, the prophet **Zoroaster** who lived in the late 1000s BCE.
Zoroastrianism is monotheistic, worshipping the god **Ahura Mazda**,
represented by fire. The Zoroastrian holy text, the **Avesta**, tells how Ahura
Mazda created the world to be good, defined by order, justice, and truth, but
was opposed by the evil Ahriman, who provided chaos. The two competed
for control of the world until an end-of-days final battle and judgement day.
Individuals had a choice to follow Ahura Mazda and would be rewarded
if they did. Zoroastrianism arose alongside Judaism, and there are many
similarities. Zoroastrianism is a living religion with most today living in Iran
and India.

CHAPTER 2

Classical Greece

THE ARCHAIC PERIOD AND TRADITIONS

Archaic Greece

This is a period (1100-776 BCE) between the end of the Myceneans and the start of the classical Greeks, sometimes known as the **Greek Dark Ages**. In this era, written scholarship and use of Linear B ended, and civilization in the Greek Isles returned to smaller village communities ruled by local strongmen that relied on subsistence farming. The historical cause of this decline is unknown. Greek accounts suggested a Mycenean civil war and subsequent invasion and conquest by a group from the north called the **Dorians**, but historical evidence for this occurrence is lacking.

The Age of Heroes

The early Greeks defined their identity and origin to a period called the Age of Heroes. They spread this knowledge through stories, which we identify as mythological literature, but the Greeks saw this as their own history. These stories included the Homeric Epics and other accounts of **demigods** who overcame great trials, such as **Theseus**, Perseus, and **Heracles**. These figures were presented as ancestors to classical Greeks. They reflected a great age that had been squandered, followed by a dark age from which humans were forced to rebuild without the aid of divine heroes. These heroes and their decline potentially reflected the archaic strongmen and a growth of dissatisfaction with this type of rule.

The Homeric Epics

The Iliad and *The Odyssey* were epic poems written by Homer about the Trojan Wars, traced to the eighth

According to The Iliad, *after years of military gridlock outside the walls of Troy, the Greeks won by trickery. Most of the Greeks sailed away, presumably ending the* siege, and they left a wooden horse, which the Trojans thought was a gift. The horse was instead filled with soldiers who proceeded to sack Troy during the night. Some scholars theorize that the **Trojan Horse** was a literary stand-in for a real-life battering ram, a boat, or a natural disaster such as a tsunami.

century BCE. Details about Homer are sparse, and some scholars argue it was an attributed name to what were oral histories, or it was the occupational name of a travelling storyteller. *The Iliad* tells the story of the Greek invasion of Troy to reclaim **Helen** who had abandoned her husband, the king of Sparta, for **Paris**, who was the prince of Troy. It details key points of conflict through epic heroes such as the demigod **Achilles**. *The Odyssey* describes the adventures of **Odysseus** as he tries to return home after the war.

Literature or History?

Modern scholars long treated the heroic texts as literature, but there is some evidence that they may have been based on real events, albeit mythologized. The most prominent example is the city of Troy. This city was believed to be a mythical location until an amateur archaeologist named **Heinrich Schliemann** bucked conventional wisdom and discovered its location. Archaeological evidence shows that the city was sacked around the time attributed to the story. Due to the lack of hard evidence, we can only speculate about the actual historical events from which the epics derive. They could reflect the war that ended Mycenean civilization, accounts of the raids of the Sea People, or perhaps another conflict.

Classical Greece

The classical Greeks consolidated culturally by 800 BCE, as they reconnected with the outside world to build their civilization, and adopted techniques such as the Phoenician alphabet and ship design, Lydian coinage, Egyptian art and architecture, and Babylonian math. The Greeks colonized new cities across the Aegean, Southern Italy, Anatolia, and the Black Sea, and they created a Greek diaspora around the Mediterranean. Although common culturally, the Greeks did not form a single political unit, instead they adopted the city-state model.

. . . .

Heinrich Schliemann is sometimes referred to as "the father of modern archaeology," and gained credit for bucking conventional wisdom to discover Troy. Nevertheless, he was reckless in his practices. Schliemann skipped over archaeological layers of the city, which had been rebuilt multiple times, and destroyed valuable remains. The layer he settled on was older than the era of the Trojan War, so he likely destroyed remains from his precise area of interest!

GREEK MILITARY CULTURE

Greek Hoplites

The heroic epics reflect how the Greeks were, in part, a martial society. Their city centers were an **acropolis**, a strategically located hilltop fortress, and military service was a key requirement of citizenship. Most Greek armies were made from volunteers, and up to 50 percent of the male population for each state was expected to answer the call to arms. Their armor featured a large round shield called a hoplon, which was a breastplate and helm supplemented by an 8-foot spear and a short sword. Greek soldiers mastered a formation called the **phalanx**. It was a tight formation with soldiers in the front holding shields while those behind held spears and provided force to the front. This formation created a wall of armor and spears, like a giant porcupine. If a man in front died, the man in the next row moved forward to maintain the formation.

Greco-Persian Wars

The First War - The classical Greeks built a rivalry with the great empire of their age, the Persians. By around 500 BCE, the **Ionian Greeks** in Anatolia were conquered to become the western edge of Persia. When the Ionian city Milesia led a revolt, Athens sent them support. They destroyed the regional Persian capital, Sardis. The Persian King **Darius I** proceeded to crush the Ionian revolt and then targeted Athens in retribution. As the largest empire in the world, Persia mustered hundreds of thousands of soldiers against the less populous and divided Greeks. The Athenians resisted the invasion at the **Battle of Marathon** in 490 BCE. The Athenian General **Miltiades** led a surprise attack against unprepared, overconfident Persians on the beaches and forced a Persian retreat. Knowing the Persians would return better prepared, Athens committed to building a navy of over 200 warships.

- -

To be successful, the phalanx relied on soldiers working in tandem and maintaining formation. This contrasts with many Hollywood movies about the Greeks, which regularly show soldiers breaking formation to pursue one-on-one combat.

The Second War - Ten years later, in 480 BCE, King **Xerxes I**, Darius' son, decided to avenge their prior defeat in Greece. He personally led an army of 200,000 troops across the **Hellespont**. This time, the Greek states unified to meet them, forming an alliance called the **Hellenic League**. Once again, the Persians dominated early, conquering much of Northern Greece. Nonetheless, a group of 6,000 men, led by Spartan king **Leonidas**, gave their lives at the mountain pass at **Thermopylae** to delay the ground forces. Leonidas and 300 Spartans, along with 600 Thespians, made a last stand to allow the others to escape. Xerxes proceeded to destroy an abandoned Athens. Led by **Themistocles**, the Athenians engaged the Persian navy in the naval **Battle of Salamis**, an island where the Athenians had relocated. While Xerxes personally watched from a hilltop, the Greeks decimated the Persian fleet. Xerxes' forces lacked logistics without their ships, and most were forced to retreat. The Greeks defeated the remaining Persian forces at the **Battle of Plataea**.

How was this possible? - The Persian strength lay in its cavalry, but chariots were difficult to use in the rocky Greek terrain. Additionally, the many natural checkpoints in Greece, such as at Thermopylae, helped mitigate Persian numbers. Additionally, the phalanx was devastating against cavalry, as horses generally do not impale themselves on spears. The naval campaign was decisive. The Persians had over 600 ships, but the quality of Greek **triremes**, built on the Phoenician model with three layers of rowers and sails, were quicker with effective rams and better-trained marines. Persian leaders afterwards found it acceptable to contain the Greeks and meddle with their politics from the outside.

Peloponnesian War

Despite the unification against Persia, military conflict remained common between the city-states. As Athens became wealthier and more powerful, it began forcing its allies to pay tribute and adopt Athenian style democracy.

*According to accounts, after the Battle of Marathon, the Athenian solider **Pheidippides** ran to Athens to spread word of their victory. This becomes the basis for the Marathon race, which is roughly 26 miles, the equivalent distance from Marathon to Athens. The story says that Pheidippides ran so hard and fast he keeled over dead upon arrival.*

This approach resulted in the Peloponnesian War between Athens and Sparta from 431-404 BCE, with the other city-states rallying to each side. In this conflict, Sparta dominated by land and Athens dominated by sea. **Pericles** decided to avoid land engagements, remaining in fortified locations, while the Spartans ravaged the countryside unopposed. Meanwhile, Athens raided Sparta from the coast and sparked a slave revolt. When Athens made a bold decision to attack the heavily fortified city of **Syracuse** in Sicily, its forces were wiped out. This result sparked a civil war over control of Athens. Sparta took advantage and destroyed what was left of the Athenian navy at port. After suffering a military occupation, Athens was left a shell of its former peak.

Spartan Hegemony and Response

The Spartans dominated the post-war period politically, and they were domineering toward their former enemies and allies alike, leading Corinth to turn against them in the **Corinthian War**. Sparta maintained its power over Greece, but its approach undermined its sustainability. The Spartans suffered high casualties, and by focusing on military pursuits, they suffered extensive population decline. In the 370s BCE, **Thebes** led a resistance, led by Epaminondas, testing new phalanx tactics. The Thebans defeated Sparta and freed their slaves, which decimated Sparta's economy. Repeating the pattern, Thebes became abusive, which led Athens to turn against it. This perpetual warfare left no city in a dominant position and decimated Greece from within.

> *The Greeks, especially the historian **Herodotus**, used the Persian King Xerxes as an example of one of their cardinal sins: hubris, or excessive self-confidence. For example, when he crossed the Hellespont on a makeshift bridge made of boats, Xerxes had his men whip the water due to a storm that destroyed one of their bridges.*

GREEK GOVERNMENT

City-State Culture and Government

The Greeks maintained a unique political system for their time, based around the model of the city-state. There were almost 1,000 independent Greek city-states, although we know very little about most of them. These states governed the agricultural land and smaller villages surrounding them. For example, the region of Attica was the rural land under the jurisdiction and citizenship of Athens. This model rejected a centralized empire over all Greeks and instead prioritized each state being unique in social structure and government. For example, Athens prioritized intellectual pursuits and art. **Corinth,** which controlled the land bridge between the main northern and southern Greek Islands, defined itself as an economic powerhouse and was known for its luxuries. **Sparta** was a warrior society organized on a military hierarchy. With a strict honor code, all male citizens were required to serve in the military and perpetually train for combat.

Spartan Soldier

Common Culture - With Greek cities and settlements stretching from Spain to the Black Sea, linked in a mutually beneficial trade network, the European Mediterranean became culturally Greek. Despite their divided governance, the Greeks had a cultural identity that we now call the **Hellenic culture**, with a common religion, art, and literature. "Hellenes" was the Greek name for themselves, although most individuals identified with his or her home city. The Greeks spoke a common language, although with different dialects. They participated in common

Athens *is the most well-known city because it had the most professional writers whose writings have survived. Accordingly, much of our knowledge of Greek history is shaped by the Athenian perspective. We know comparatively little about most of the other Greek cities.*

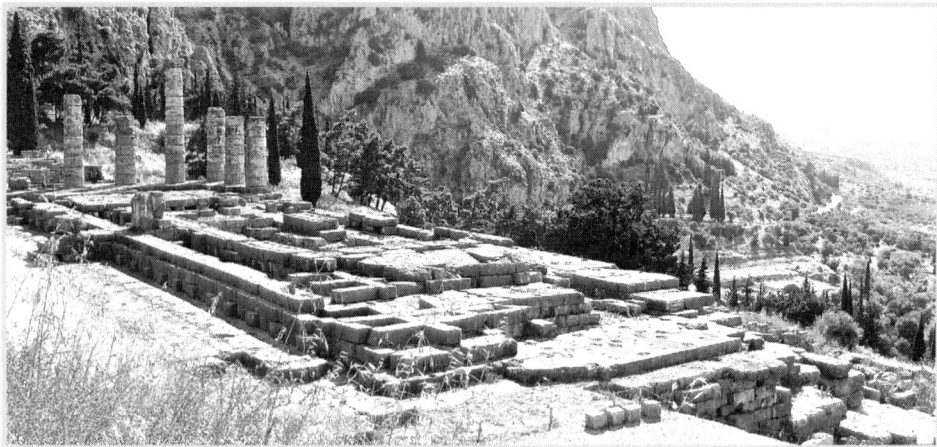

Temple of Apollo at Delphi

cultural activities such as visiting the **Temple of Apollo at Delphi**, where Greeks made pilgrimages to seek advice from the **oracle**. Competitions of all sorts became a routine, including sports. The **Olympics** were founded in 776 BCE to honor Zeus, and they were held in the city of Olympia. The Olympics became a peaceful way for rival city-states to compete. Competitions also took place for theater, music, and poetry, and were held at regular festivals.

The Polis

Another commonality arose in the idea that a Greek city-state, which was called a *polis*, should be ruled by the body of citizens rather than by detached rulers. The citizenry participated in determining the best laws, organizing justice, and selecting leaders. City-states embraced this concept, although each differed in form. Some were oligarchies which were led by small councils; others were democracy, which followed a large government council; and other elected an individual ruler, who my well be tyrannical. The Greek states mixed these forms among them, and some shifted in different points in their history.

*The Greeks believed that the **Temple at Delphi**, having been built upon the stone that Kronos ate and subsequently disgorged, was a direct link to the gods. The **Oracle at Delphi** was a priestess who received vague predictions after eating volcanic ash.*

Athenian Democracy

To illustrate Athenian democracy, Athens started as an oligarchy ruled by a group of nine elites called the archons. The archons served as an executive council appointed by an aristocratic city council. The archon **Dracon** established the first written law, but his civic order by enforced a harsh system. A revolution against this system put **Solon** in power as the lone archon. He implemented reforms that established a new council, the **ekklesia**, in which all property-owning men could run for office and all citizens chose representatives. The ekklesia then chose new archons. The Athenian government also included courts overseen by elected representatives. After a brief return to tyranny, the politician **Cleisthenes** established reforms that reorganized voting districts and diverted power away from aristocrats and into local communities. In the 400s BCE, Pericles pushed greater democracy. New laws established payments for poorer citizens to join government activities and allowed the ekklesia and public referendums to propose new laws. Elected generals, called *strategos*, became the chief executives and the most powerful figures in government.

Other Models

Tyrannies were often popular in city-states. For example, **Periander** in Corinth ruled in the late 600s BCE as an absolute dictator. He did, however, cut taxes, sponsor development of the trireme, and begin coining money. He became identified as an exemplar of the **philosopher king**, who cut through political morass to achieve important goals. Tyrannies were expected to be temporary and to return to plural rule. The model of the oligarchy was also common, connected to ruling aristocracies. Sparta, for example, had a dual monarchy of two leading aristocratic families. It also maintained a separation of powers, with an assembly where Spartans over 30 could serve and vote, and an executive council where those over 60 were elected. Each body had its own roles and powers.

* * *

*To challenge Sparta, Theban General Epaminondas formed the **Theban Sacred Band**, a professional military unit who gave up their everyday lives entirely to serve as full-time soldiers. They helped lead Thebes to dominance in Greece until the forces of **Philip of Macedon** defeated and killed the entire band.*

GREEK ECONOMY AND SOCIETY

Economic and Social Shift

Trade was an essential part of the Greek economy as their food production did not meet population growth. In Athens, Solon drove an economic shift to grapes and olives as cash crops, oil and wine production, pottery manufacturing, and silver mining. These goods were traded in exchange for grain and luxury goods. This approach saw economic prosperity. As the Greeks improved on the Phoenician model of ships by making them lighter and more maneuverable, they displaced the Phoenician's control over Eastern Mediterranean trade. A large, open-air marketplace, called an *agora*, featured anything available at the time. As the scale of economies rose, cities began adopting coin money as a common transfer. Corinthian and Athenian silver coins became the common currency of exchange. '

Helots

The big exception was Sparta, which saw economic pursuits as a distraction. They maintained a plantation agricultural system that used a slave population called "helots" and a group of free, non-citizen farmers recruited from other Greek states. Spartans comprised only five percent of their population; 15 percent were free peasants, and 80 percent were helots.

Economic Decline

The Peloponnesian War and the subsequent conflicts weakened the Greek economy. Agriculture was decimated, with grapevines and olive groves needing long periods to mature. Mass inflation, falling living standards, and mass unemployment became the norm. Many Greeks found employment

Once a year, to maintain its fighting force and to train young soldiers, Sparta declared war on the helots. This act of violence kept their soldiers engaged and the helots oppressed.

only as mercenary soldiers for the larger empires around them. In one famous case, the brother of one Persian emperor hired a group of 10,000 Greeks to overthrow the Persian government. When this failed, the Greeks were trapped deep in Persia and fought their way out, as written by one of the survivors, **Xenophon**.

Aristocracy

Socially, the Greeks maintained a hierarchical system based on an aristocracy. The term itself originally meant "rule of the best." While predominantly a title held by elite families, others could rise from the general population by gaining wealth in the market economy, by showing military prowess, or by becoming well educated. The wealthiest landowning elites sat at the top of this hierarchy, but there were status levels down to small-plot farmers. All had citizenship. The wealthy were considered the aristoi and were expected to show a model lifestyle of ethics to match their success. Hubris, or thinking too highly of oneself, became a main cause of the gods to smote someone down. Well-treatment of guests and devotion of money to the arts and toward infrastructure was a social expectation of all people.

Non-Citizens

Women did not have citizenship and were devoted to domestic life, raising children, cooking, or completing tasks such as weaving textiles. Women also played a very public role in religious ceremonies, often organizing and leading them. They also served as temple priestesses. Slaves were a normal part of Greek society and were treated as members of their master's household. Slaves served in many economic roles, including in manufacturing, and could potentially buy their own freedom. Greek cities also had free, non-citizen residents, including foreigners and freed slaves.

*The stories of the Greek gods are often very strange. For example, according to Greek mythology, **Kronos**, the leader of the **Titans**, literally ate his children (the gods) to prevent them from challenging his power. They remained alive in his stomach, because they were immortal. Zeus escaped when his mother replaced him with a stone. Zeus poisoned Kronos to make his father throw up the other gods. The gods then proceeded to overthrow Titan rule.*

Greek Religion

What we call today "Greek mythology" was a living religion for the Greeks. It featured many gods providing order by controlling some natural element. Greek mythology contained its own sense of history. Zeus and the other gods had overthrown their parents, the Titans, before regularly feuding with one another. They otherwise lived their lives on **Mount Olympus**, or elsewhere, while sometimes meddling in human affairs. Gods were essentially humans with superpowers and behaved like humans, warts and all. They become the basis of literature, as the affairs of the gods become parables for humans. Each city had a patron god, such as **Athena** for Athens. Temples were built with a statue of the god to give sacrifices as a sign of respect. Greeks were expected to worship and sacrifice to the gods or else face their wrath. There was no professional priestly class, other than oracles, who gave advice and predicted the future. City officials led religious ceremonies, and it was up to individuals to hold ceremonies when needed.

The Greek Pantheon

The Greek Pantheon referred to the collection of Greek gods led by the 12 Olympians who ruled from Mount Olympus. While the Olympic gods were the most important, there were many more Greek gods who played different roles in their mythology.

> *Sporting events at the original Olympics and other festivals included short-distance and long-distance running, boxing, upright and ground-based wrestling, and **pankration**, a mix of boxing and wrestling. Discus, javelin, and standing jump joined running and wrestling in the pentathlon. Success at the Olympics was source of great fame, often mythologized.*

Caryatids at the Parthenon in Acropolis, Athens

God	Role
Zeus	Father, King of the Gods, Thunder, Weather, Order
Hera	Mother, Queen of the Gods, Marriage, Family
Athena	Wisdom, War, Crafts
Apollo	Music, Prophecy
Poseidon	The Sea, Rivers, Earthquakes
Ares	War
Artemis	Hunting, Chastity
Demeter	Agriculture
Aphrodite	Love, Beauty
Dionysus	Wine, Theater, Festivity
Hermes	Trade, Wealth, Travel, Communication
Hephaistos	Fire, Metallurgy

Greek theater took place at celebrations such as the spring feast of Dionysus, the god of wine. Three playwrights were chosen per festival and competed for the best performance. Plays took a form where two opposing forces (protagonist and antagonist) exchanged dialogue, while a chorus in the background narrated the story and provided reactions to characters on stage.

43

Greek Academics - The lack of centralization in Greece facilitated much open discussion and debate, which led to new ideas and understandings. The ideas and scholarship of the classical Greeks set the stage for the development Western civilization.

Literature

Epics defined a concept of the past and told stories of old heroes and their interaction with the gods to teach lessons. Other works of fiction looked to entertain and teach a lesson in the form of plays, acted out in **amphitheaters**. **Aeschylus'** play *The Persians* focused on Xerxes, showing him as a tragic victim of hubris. **Sophocles** outlined the important concept of fate in his writings, as in *Oedipus Rex* for example. In the *Trojan Women*, **Euripides** showed the tragedy of warfare through the treatment of women in the sacking of Troy. Plays were established for celebrations, such as the spring feast devoted to Dionysus. Greek musicians wrote lyrics, poetic songs played with a lyre (small harp), such as those by **Sappho**.

Philosophy

In addition, individuals arose who made thinking their trade. They became known as **philosophers** from the Greek word for "love of wisdom," but in functional life served as teachers. Most of the classical philosophers addressed ethics and human society.

Socrates

Socrates was a stonemason and Peloponnesian War veteran who became a philosopher. He called for people to make decisions based on key universal principles, such as justice, virtue, and love. With larger questions open debate would take place. This gave as many perspectives as possible which

Despite his prominence, Socrates never wrote down his own teachings. Socrates' students, such as Plato and Xenophon, kept Socrates' legacy alive by publishing his teachings. For example, Plato's Socratic dialogues account for conversations between Socrates, his students, and other notable figures.

caused the best response to arise. Socrates was killed for criticizing Athenian democracy and for "corrupting the youth." Given a chance for exile, he accepted the punishment to live up to his belief in obeying the law. Socrates inspired many later philosophers that identified themselves as part of the **Socratic school** of philosophy.

Plato

One such example was Plato. When he formed his own school, the **Academy**, Plato wrote his own ideas in the voice of Socrates. In his work *Republic*, Plato argued that the ideal government is one that prioritized order and social harmony over individual liberty. He argued that a small group of intellectual elites should govern a society, as philosopher kings, who would make the best choices. This reflected Plato's view of the perfectibility of mankind. He felt that there were conceptual forms that people needed to find in their lives (perfect soldier, farmer, etc.) to build the ideal society.

Aristotle

Plato's own student, Aristotle focused on establishing clearly defined categories and methods of study. He categorized several areas of ethics (courage, temperance, etc.) and asserted that individuals should focus on moderation and balance to lead a rational life. He believed that only through freedom could man pursue his highest form, pursuing reason, but mankind needed ethics to be truly free.

Humanities

Other scholars developed ideas in the humanities, math, and sciences. These scholars attempted to study humans on their own terms, rather than in relation to the gods. Herodotus was the "first" historian. His writings served

The historians Herodotus and Thucydides showed a shift in Greek academics toward the study of human affairs independent of the gods. Whereas the gods play a key role in Herodotus' history, they are nonexistent as active characters in Thucydides' work.

Parthenon at the Acropolis in Athens, Greece

as the base of most knowledge of the Greeks but were followed by later works by historians, such as **Thucydides'** history of the Peloponnesian Wars. **Xenophon** wrote about Spartan culture, which he admired, as well as a notable book on economics.

Sciences

In the sciences, **Thales** conceptualized that water was the building block of life, and **Pythagoras** developed the Pythagorean theorem, determined even and odd numbers, and built the idea that everything should be measured by numbers. These Greek scientists expanded on the work of Near Eastern scientists and mathematicians and inspired future scholars.

Art

Where the classical Greeks were perhaps the most impressive was in their artwork. Greek architecture focused on streamlined designs, such as the elaborate **Parthenon**, commissioned by Pericles to honor Athena. **Phidias** sculpted the temple entirely with marble with a terra-cotta roof and a gold statue of Athena. Greek art, particularly sculpture, established the artistic school of **realism**. Artists attempted to show the perfected human form, such as Phidias' statue of Zeus at Olympia. This style shifted over time to show people as they appeared rather than the physical ideal of a person. Bronze became a new medium for sculpture rather than stone, as it lasted longer. It required both advanced artistry and metallurgy.

CHAPTER 3

The Hellenistic Age

Hellenistic Age

This refers to a period starting in the 300s BCE when Greek culture spread rapidly and blended with other cultures in the Mediterranean and Western Asia. In this era, the decentralized structure of the Greek city-states came to an end and was replaced by large Greek empires. The Greeks came to dominate the Eastern Mediterranean and the Near East until the consolidation of the Roman Empire in the first century BCE.

Macedonia

This outcome occurred due to the actions of a hereto marginal people in Northern Greece called the Macedonians. During the classical age, Macedonia featured a poorer society, made up of people living mostly in small villages, despite a well-developed capital city at Aegae. Unlike the other Greeks, Macedonia had a permanent, hereditary kingship. Macedonian leaders were eager for acceptance by the other Greeks, who treated them as a marginally barbaric people. They spoke Greek, but in a unique dialect, and received marginal participation in other Greek affairs. To gain status, Macedonian rulers paid important scholars to visit them, such as the poet Euripides. Macedonia had great economic potential with minerals, timber, and agriculture but remained distracted by internal and external conflict.

Philip II of Macedon

In the mid-fourth century, Philip, the youngest son of the king, became a **ward** at Thebes where he received a quality education and military training. When he gained power unexpectedly, Philip trained his forces in the Theban style, until it had among the best phalanxes in Greece. The Macedonian phalanx adapted by using 16-foot pikes, supplemented by a cavalry able

· ·

While the Macedonian kings paid important scholars to visit them to build credibility, this sometimes backfired. For example, the poet Euripides died there when mauled by Macedonian hunting dogs.

Artwork of Alexander the Great in Battle

to move at a comparatively rapid pace. After conquering the **Southern Balkans**, Philip cultivated its gold mines. It allowed him to hire Aristotle to teach his son Alexander and afforded Macedonia funds for additional military campaigns. The Athenian orator **Isocrates** encouraged Philip to consider waging a new war against Persia to unite the Greeks. When Athens and other Greek cities rejected this idea, he decided to unify them through conquest. By 330 BCE, Philip conquered Athens and Thebes after the **Battle of Chaeronea**, while forcing the submission of the other Greek states. He did not achieve his broader goals, however, and was assassinated.

Alexander the Great

Philip's ambitious 20-year-old son Alexander took over this new Greek empire in 356 BCE. Adopting his father's mission, Alexander III went on the offensive against Persia, facing off against Emperor **Darius III**. Despite being outnumbered, Alexander's forces conquered Ionia, winning battle after battle. When Darius led forces personally against Alexander at the **Battle of Issus River**, Alexander got the heavily armored Persian forces boxed against the muddy riverbanks, while his lighter, quicker troops cleaned up against

- -

Few expected Philip II to rule Macedonia. Sent away to Thebes as an after-thought, he took power only when his two older brothers died, one in battle and the other when assassinated, a common fate for Macedonian leaders. Philip ran with the opportunity and built alliances among Macedonian nobles and neigh-boring tribes to consolidate his authority.

Sculpture of Alexander the Great

them. Unabated, he drove his forces into the Near East, conquering many historical cities. He faced Darius again, for the final time, at the **Battle of Gaugamela** in Mesopotamia, coming out victorious. Within two years, his forces had conquered Persia and took the royal titles of all the historical kingdoms (Persia, Akkad, Sumer, and Egypt). Alexander's forces then conquered the Central Asian trading hub of **Bactria** and made it as far as the Indus River. Alexander died at the age of 32 after falling ill and refusing to rest, believing himself invulnerable.

Alexandria

When Alexander marched into Egypt, the Egyptians welcomed him without a fight and declared him the new pharaoh. As the Greeks admired Egyptian civilization, Alexander decided to establish his new capital in Egypt, founding the city of Alexandria in 332 BCE.

*During his campaigns, Alexander rode his beloved horse, **Bucephalus**. Alexander was said to have tamed the wild horse as a boy. Bucephalus fell in battle in what is now Pakistan. When founding new cities, Alexander always named them after himself, with one exception. He named one city after Bucephalus following the horse's death.*

THE HELLENISTIC EMPIRES

Alexander's Expanded Empire

Although a great conqueror, Alexander's vast empire did not last long. He implemented no formal ruling organization nor a clear successor. After two years of civil war, his generals divided and ruled his conquests as separate empires.

Ptolemaic Egypt

In Egypt, the general Ptolemy took control, realizing its cultural significance. Ptolemy had Alexander's body entombed in Alexandria, making it a pilgrimage site. In the era of Ptolemaic Egypt, all subsequent pharaohs were named Ptolemy, and their sisters named **Cleopatra**, the name of Alexander's sister. Greeks served as the ruling class but maintained the traditional Egyptian civil service, who ran the day-to-day affairs of the empire. The longest lasting of the empires, Alexandria became the new cultural center of the Mediterranean. The Ptolemies commissioned creation of the **Library of Alexandria** and **Museum of Alexandria** and financed much new scholarship.

Seleucid Persia

General Seleucus took control of Persia and used his Persian wife to claim a new imperial line. His son Antiochus then established a new capital closer to the Mediterranean at Antioch in Syria. He traded the eastern portions of the empire to make it more manageable. Consolidating in Syria, its emperors, the Seleucids, copied the Persian administrative method, which relied on local leaders and bureaucracies to maintain control. The empire grew its wealth through trade, facilitating the transfer of luxury goods between Central and South Asia and the Mediterranean. The empire developed cities

When Alexander's funeral cart left Babylon headed for Macedonia, it was seized by Ptolemy I and diverted to Egypt where it was temporarily in Memphis and then removed to Alexandria for burial. However, there is still controversy about whether the person entombed in Alexandria is truly Alexander the Great, and the current location of Alexander's tomb is probably unknown.

51

along the route, such as Palmyra, to facilitate this trade. Geographically unwieldy, the eastern part of the empire fractured after a group called the **Parthians** in Western Iran gained independence, and it regularly lost territory around its margins, gradually declining in size during the Hellenistic era.

Antigonid Greece

General Antigonus took control of Greece and Macedonia. During this period, Macedon remained a kingdom and ruled Greece through a system that paid homage to the classical model of Greek government. There remained a few nominally independent states, such as Sparta, and Greek administration was reorganized into regional confederations, the two largest being the **Aetolian League** and the **Achaean League**. These leagues established a federalist framework called *koinon*. The city-states maintained their own governments, but a larger federal government, led by an elected council, developed common programs, notably military and foreign policy. The city-states and koinon functionally ruled Greece, while the Antigonids provided oversight of the region and could overrule the regional bodies. These factions fought with one another constantly over territory, but due to having relatively equal status, little changed among them.

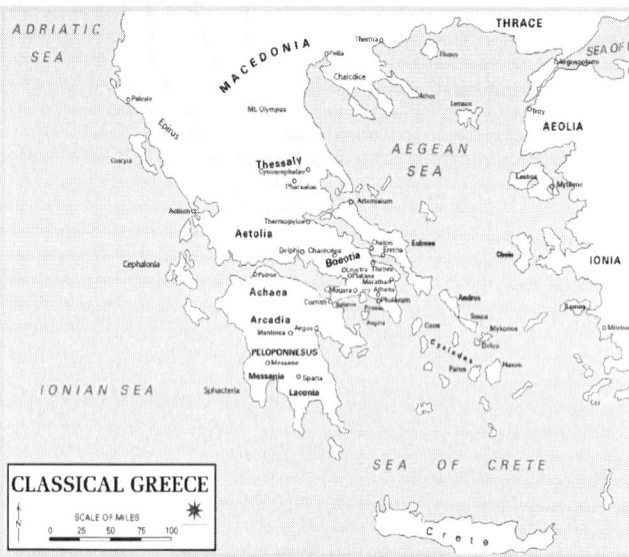

Map of Classical Greece

After his victories, Alexander the Great insisted upon being treated like a living god. He declared himself the son of Zeus, and the equivalent to epic heroes such as Heracles and Achilles. He later made his men worship him in the style of Persian rulers, and accounts suggest they came to resent him by the end of his life. His death perhaps reflects the Greek sin of hubris.

HELLENISTIC CULTURE

Expansion of Greek Culture

The biggest impact of Alexander's conquest was cultural. Alexander made a concentrated effort to spread Greek culture abroad as a means of stabilizing his empire. In doing so, Alexander replaced the old Greek polis system with a *cosmopolis*. This was to be a large, multiethnic empire based on Greek culture but one in which citizen participation in government was mostly gone. Alexander was given a god-like status, and his successors became detached rulers, separated from the common person as figures of worship.

Economics

Alexander absorbed the vast stores of treasure from Persian elites, which caused an economic boom throughout the Mediterranean. It also sparked a mass expansion of slavery as conquered people were sold off as rewards. Huge plantations were established by the wealthy who purchased most of the agriculturally viable areas and disenfranchised former owners who had to find new lives in cities. Alexander's empire also linked Central Asia with the Mediterranean trade network, establishing a 5,000 mile trade zone that became the western half of the **Silk Road**, a vast trade network that at its peak stretched from Britain to China. Countless goods of all kinds transferred along these routes for thousands of years afterwards. By 100 BCE, the Hellenistic region was using commonly exchanged coin money.

Greeks relied on a variety of foods. Wheat was their staple and used to make bread. They also relied on a variety of beans and chickpeas as well as fruits, such as olives, figs, and pomegranates. Vegetables, such as carrots and onions, were used to make soups. Dairy and fish were common, while meat was reserved for the wealthy. They ate a type of pancake, called tiganites, with honey and regularly drank wine.

Alexander pursued the largest military seizure of wealth until the discovery of the Americas. While we do not know the exact amount seized and relocated to Greece, Alexander's conquest sparked an economic revival in Greece.

Urbanization

Alexander himself founded 70 new cities; his successors, 200 more. These cities were to be cultural and economic hubs, as Alexander relocated people from across the empire to populate them. Alexandria, Egypt, was built from scratch in this way and soon reached a half million population. Alexander and his successors had Greeks relocate to new parts of the empire by granting them farmland, and he had them marry wives from the local population. These Greek migrants became the ruling class and the vehicle for the spread of Greek culture.

Cultural Assimilation

Alexander had common Greek established as a lingua franca to allow people in the diverse empire to communicate and share culture. Classical Greek culture, such as art, education, science, philosophy, architecture, and entertainment, spread throughout the region. While the Library at Alexandria was the largest, libraries and monuments were built in many other cities. Across the Hellenistic world, Greek culture blended with local cultures of different regions. One such example was the state of Bactria, where Hellenistic and Central Asian culture blended and survived as the core culture there long after Alexander's death. Greek purity was replaced with **syncretism**, the blending of cultures, and Greek culture spread abroad with other cultures spreading to Greece.

Religious Syncretism and Mystery Cults

Religion is a key example of syncretism. Greek gods spread throughout Asia, with many temples built to honor them, while gods from other religions spread into Greece. Many of the gods saw their stories and depictions blended into new hybrids. For example, the new sun god Serapis arose as a hybrid of the Egyptian god Amun and Zeus. Babylonian astrology, based

*In Central Asia, Greek culture met and blended with the Buddhist religion, which originated in northern India. This **Greco-Buddhism** developed in Bactria and neighboring kingdoms and is seen in philosophy and art. A king in Graeco-India, **Menander I Soter**, was a Greek who converted to Buddhism and became a key sage.*

on predicting events along the stars, gained extensive popularity in Greece, as did beliefs that mystical objects could be used to gain a god's personal favor. Cults worshipping individual gods, such as the Dionysus cult, Isis cult, and Cybele cult, arose across the empires. People believed that if they maintained rituals honoring a god, they would come to live alongside that god when they died.

Opposition to Assimilation

Many cultures embraced the changes, but others resisted. In the Western Mediterranean, the Romans and Carthaginians embraced many components of Hellenistic culture, such as art, literature, and religion, but fiercely asserted their political independence. The Persians had previously embraced religious tolerance, and many Zoroastrians responded to the pressures to conform for Greek religion by calling on people to reject the material world and Hellenization and to live as aesthetics to purify their souls. The new Hellenistic order also greatly challenged the Jewish populations. Some of the Jewish populations embraced Hellenistic customs. They learned the Greek language, culture, and philosophy, although many maintained their own faith. They translated the Hebrew Bible into Greek. Other Jewish groups called for Jewish purity and rejection of Greek culture. The **Maccabees** rebelled against this influence and formed an independent city-state at Jerusalem after Antiochus IV Epiphanes outlawed their faith. An army led by **Judas** won the ensuing battle to make Jerusalem a free city-state. This event is honored by the Jewish holiday **Hanukkah**.

Hanukkah Menorah

Hanukkah is a Jewish holiday marking the re-sanctification of the **Second Temple** after the **Maccabean Revolt**. The menorah honors a miracle where candles with only enough wick and oil for one day instead burned for eight days.

HELLENISTIC ACADEMICS

Philosophy

The religious fervor of the Hellenistic age saw a counterreaction in new philosophies that argued for the existence of a completely material world. **Stoicism**, developed by Zeno of Citium, argued that the world worked like a big machine and that all an individual could do would be to choose how to respond to events and free one's mind to accept things. The scholar **Epicurus** took a similar approach (**Epicurism**), but he decided that the universe was random and disorderly with no human purpose. One should just live a joyful life based on personal happiness, avoiding pain, until death. The **skeptics**, led by Carneades, believed that since people perceive everything through their senses, one cannot really know anything. One should just seek a peace of mind by not believing anything and just living the best life possible.

*Hippocrates developed much knowledge of medical practices from his school on Kos at a massive temple devoted to Asclepios, the god of healing. He is also known for the **Hippocratic Oath**, a pledge not to harm the patient through treatment that is still recognized by doctors today.*

Science

This period also saw a boom in the sciences. Alexander brought scientists with him during his conquests, and the blending of cultures allowed a rapid sharing of ideas and scientific understanding. **Aristarchus of Samos** established that the Earth revolved around the sun. **Euclid** and **Hipparchus** organized formal geometry and trigonometry, respectively. **Eratosthenes** in Alexandria calculated the size of Earth almost perfectly. **Archimedes** in Syracuse developed many engineering feats, including pulleys and levers, a device for pumping water for irrigation,

*The head librarian at Alexandria, **Zenodotus**, established an organization of texts by subject matter, then author, a system still used in libraries today. The Library at Alexandria collected scholarship from across the Hellenistic world to make the library the intellectual and cultural center of the age, with many premier scholars moving there.*

and a propeller used mostly in construction and naval pursuits. He also discovered how floating works. **Ctesibius** and **Hero** developed air pressure and water pressure devices, respectively. These techniques were used to make early machines, such as toys and clocks. Hippocrates recognized diet as a cause of illness and set standard practices of medical ethics and treatment.

The Arts

The same surge occurred with art, as wealthy patrons devoted resources toward new works. Cities commissioned new archaeological wonders, such as the **Citadel**, the **Lighthouse of Alexandria**, and the **Colossus of Rhodes**. Literature continued to flourish. The poet **Theocritus** focused on escapism and wrote about leaving urban trappings to enjoy life in the countryside. **Polybius** became the prominent historian and wrote about the rise of Rome. He developed the idea of life cycles of empires and believed that all such followed similar patterns and lifespans.

Lighthouse of Alexandria
Drawing by Archaeologist Hermann Thiersch

*The Lighthouse of Alexandria, one of the **Seven Wonders of the Ancient World**, was one of the tallest standing buildings of the ancient world. It utilized a mirror to reflect sunlight to guide ships during the day and a fire hearth at night. It was destroyed by an earthquake and no longer exists.*

*Archimedes discovered how floating works while taking a bath. He supposedly jumped out of his bath and ran through the streets naked shouting "eureka," meaning "I have found it." He is also believed to have invented an early computer, used to chart the movement of the planets, called the **Antikythera mechanism**.*

CHAPTER 4

The Roman Republic

CLASSICAL EUROPE AND EARLY ROME

Classical Europe

While the classical Greek and the Hellenistic age left significant cultural and economic influences on Europe, it changed the political situation in Europe very little beyond Greece. The rest of Europe remained divided among many groups that competed with one another with no dominant empire until the rise of the Roman Empire in the first century.

The Celts - Between 1000 to 250 BCE, there was a mass migration of a people called the Celts. While their starting point is disputed, Celtic peoples settled throughout much of Europe, stretching from Eastern Europe to Spain and the British Isles. They maintained a common culture in language, art, and religion, although they were divided politically among many tribal groups. Each tribe was led by a king, and he used a warrior council whose leaders were chosen based on charisma and effectiveness in battle. Celtic tribes regularly harassed the city-states along the Mediterranean coastline. They had probably the best quality iron weapons in Europe and developed the first chainmail.

Celtic Economy

Advanced agriculturally, the Celtic tribes also participated in the Mediterranean trade networks, linking them to their own networks along the Danube and Rhine Rivers. Celtic tribes became wealthy while working as middlemen for this trade and by mining iron. They produced ornate artwork, particularly in metalworking and glass. The Celtics established the first cities in Europe located in the north of the Alps. Many current location names likely have their origin in the Celtic language, such as London and Paris.

*Celtic **Druids** purportedly had the power to imbue items with special powers. One example were gold neck rings believed to dissipate fear in battle. Accounts have Celtic warriors fighting naked, wearing only these rings.*

Celtic Religion

The Celtic religion was naturalist. Gods represented elements of the natural world, and different tribes prioritized and worshipped different individual gods. Their religion was directed to an 'otherworld,' where gods, spirits of the dead, and other mystical creatures lived. These beings could sometimes reach into the living world and interact with it. Certain regions offered a crossing point to the spiritual world, such as caves, bogs, and forests. Their religious leaders were called the Druids. The Druids' role as the educated class was to communicate with the spirit world and natural phenomena to get directions, shape the climate, and imbue items with power from gods.

Pre-Roman Italy

Italy was not the ideal starting point for an empire. Italy had timber, marble, and good agricultural land, although fewer natural harbors for trade compared to Greece. Its northern portion was dominated by the **Etruscans**, a non-Indo-European people who had migrated from Anatolia. They appear to have ruled through a confederation of city-states while ruling over several other non-Etruscan cities, including Rome. Adept at metalworking, they were part of the Mediterranean trade networks through close contact with the Greeks who controlled southern Italy. Rome derived much of its culture from them, such as religious ceremonies and gladiatorial combat. The Etruscans helped to urbanize Rome and to build infrastructures, such as the Roman Forum. There were other peoples in Italy who identified independently, such as the Latins, Sabines, and Samnites, identified commonly as the **Italics**.

Celtic Invasions

Celtic tribes crossed over the Alps and succeeding in conquering parts of northern Italy in the early 300s BCE. This invasion severely weakened the Etruscans, and the other Italians came under threat. At the **Battle of Allia**

*The holiday of Halloween has its roots in an ancient Celtic holiday called **Samhain**. The Celts believed that because this period marked the start of the dark period of the year, the veil was lifted on the otherworld and allowed creatures from there to interact with the living. Celtic villages collected at large bonfires for protection on this night.*

in 390 BCE, the Romans engaged Celtic tribes for the first time. The Celts, led by Brennus, defeated the Roman forces and sacked Rome. Rome, led by **Marcus Camillus**, later fought off this invasion and refortified the city. Galvanized by this event, they set up the **Servian Wall**, and refocused their society around military service. This period set the stage for the Romans to become the dominant power in Italy.

Roman Origin Story

Originally founded in the 700s BCE, Rome began as a city-state like the Greek model. The Romans had several origin stories passed down via oral history and later codified. The Romans claimed to be ancestors of the Trojan hero **Aeneas** who led the surviving Trojans to Italy where they joined with the Latins. Aeneas' ancestors, **Romulus** and **Remus** were orphaned, and their uncle, a usurper king, tried to have them killed. They were sent down the Tiber River by a sympathetic executioner, suckled by a wolf, and found and raised by a shepherd. Upon discovering their origins, Romulus and Remus founded a city and populated it with Latins and Sabines. Romulus ended up murdering Remus over a political dispute and became the first of seven kings of the eponymous Rome.

Roman Historical Origin

Historians have determined that the Romans began as part of the Latins, an Indo-European people who migrated into Italy from the Balkans. Rome began as a small village, speaking the **Latin** language. Their location in central Italy along the Tiber River allowed them to become a hub for trade between the Greeks, Latins, and the Etruscans. Although a city-state, they were part of a Latin confederation. Much like the Greeks, the Latin states regularly fought, but they also cooperated based on the system of **Latin right**, which guaranteed free trade, intermarriage, and citizenship between all Latin cities. The Latins had close links with the Greeks and received much culture from them, including their alphabet, art and architecture, their religion, and hero literature. Greek gods had Roman equivalents as did the ancient heroes, such as the Greek Heracles who became the Roman **Hercules**.

* * *

*Although a prominent society in ancient Italy, most knowledge of the **Etruscans** comes from Roman sources. The Etruscans spoke a pre-Indo-European language, which has not yet been translated.*

ROMAN SOCIETY AND GOVERNMENT

Social Structure

Under the Republic, the Romans defined themselves as a society of farmers and chastised city life. They maintained a strict societal honor code called the *mos maiorum* meaning code of the elders. This code set Roman cultural standards, such as patriotism, responsibility, frugality, temperance, and modesty. Another component was piety to family elders. Death masks of ancestors were hung on walls after funerals, and names reflected lineage to past ancestors of great achievement. Families without sons or daughters could adopt to continue the family legacy. Women managed the household with their primary expectation to have children but also maintained a public role by hosting social gatherings. Women also had rights to control property and petition for divorce.

Government

Rome was originally led by kings and advised by a council of elders called the **Senate**. Roman history stated that the Etruscans placed kings over them before the Romans overthrew them and committed never to return to a monarchy. Their government was identified as the *res publica* meaning the public body. This model, now called a republic, was based on multiple, divided forms of government designed to compete with one another to limit total power by an individual or group. Some positions in Roman government were popularly elected, but others were appointed. Roman citizenship granted the rights of property ownership, marriage, and jurisdiction under Roman law. Men could vote and run for office. Children only gained citizenship if both parents had it. Slaves and foreigners lacked such rights.

> *Roman society expected extreme levels of honor and subservience to the head of the household, or the* **pater familias**. *A father had almost complete authority over his family members. This mentality was illustrated in the story of* **Aeneas** *carrying his elderly father on his back out of Troy.*

Roman Government

The Roman Republic was a complex system, with powers divided between many individuals and councils of different sizes.

Consuls

Roman citizens voted on two consuls every year to lead the military and carry out the will of the Republic. The consuls were the chief executives, and each consul had veto power over the other.

The Senate

The consuls nominated people to the Senate to serve life terms. The Senate was a council of 300-600 officials which had lawmaking power and oversight over the many executive offices, including veto power over executive decisions. Leadership in the Senate was chosen based on a vote that ranked each senator, with the first being the **princep**.

Other Roles

Rome did not allow people to serve as both businessmen and politicians, so those serving in business became the **equestrian order**. They used their money to support the military cavalry. They also aided politicians who had given up moneymaking, and gradually gained powers, such as managing Roman taxes. Several other executive officials were elected, including **praetors** (chief lawyers), aediles (markets and city infrastructure overseers), quaestors (financial officers), censors (tax collectors and census takers), among many others. Other assemblies, such as the tribal assembly or centurion assembly, would be called to guide a direct vote on an issue from the citizenry. When Rome conquered new territory, these provinces did not gain citizenship, and a proconsul (governor) was appointed to manage finances, collect taxes, and administer courts of the territory.

Patricians and Plebeians

Initially, only the aristocratic class, known as the patricians, served as senators. The patricians were an inherited aristocracy who claimed to have descended from famous ancestors. They had first vote in the Senate, ran the courts, and initially had a monopoly on knowledge of the law, passed down orally through families. By the late Republic, a new form of politician arose, chosen from popular assemblies, called the plebeians, or plebs. The plebs were people of common birth, making up 98 percent of the Roman citizenry, ranging from wealthy merchants, to small plot farmers, to poor laborers. These two factions regularly feuded in the **Struggle of the Orders**. Reforms gradually expanded plebeian authority, allowing them to elect tribunes to represent a directly elected plebeian assembly. The tribunes negotiated with patricians and voted to support executive decisions. The assembly later gained the power to write laws applying only to plebeians. If affirmed by the Senate, these laws applied to all of Rome.

The Law of Twelve Tables

This was the first fully written Roman legal code and ended the patrician monopoly on legal knowledge. While it covered all aspects of the law, it also gave the plebs full rights in the Senate and legalized marriage between the two orders.

Roman Dictators

In times of crises, particularly war, Rome would accept a dictator. Seen as a positive figure, this dictator ruled with complete power to provide decisive leadership until the crises ended. The model for this role became **Cincinnatus**. This Roman general reluctantly became dictator to win a war. He then relinquished power and returned to his farm.

George Washington was often compared to Cincinnatus due to his similar reluctance for politics, and the Society of Cincinnatus formed as an organization of veterans of the American Revolution. The city of Cincinnati is derived from this name.

Roman Religion

The Roman gods were the first fathers and mothers, although they were treated with fewer human qualities than their Greek equivalents. The Romans honored them in rituals, such as animal sacrifices on the **Capitoline Hill** temple for **Jupiter**. Roman Senators served rotations as priests, leading ceremonies and offering advice in the temples. The *pontifex maximus* was the head priest. He oversaw the other priests and the **Vestal Virgins** who kept the **hearth fire of Vesta** burning at the **Roman Forum** and controlled the calendar. The Romans embraced the Greek gods, although they had many unique gods outside of the primary pantheon.

*The **Vestal Virgins**, who maintained the hearth fire at the Temple of Vesta, held the most honored religious role for women. They were chosen between the age of six and 10, and they served for 30 years. The Vestal Virgins could marry only when their service was up, and one who broke chastity would be buried alive.*

Roman Forum

The Roman Forum was the center of Roman civic life. Government activities, voting, criminal trials, public speeches, and triumphs took place here. It was also the location of the most important temples.

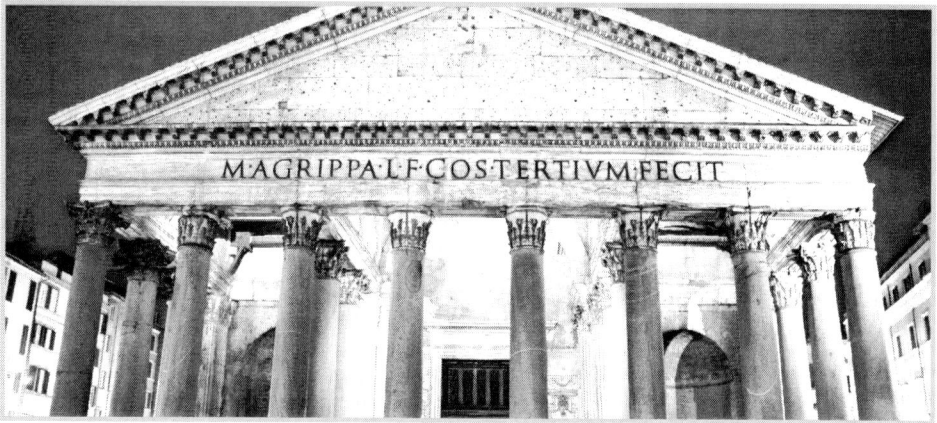

Pantheon in Rome, Italy

Roman God	Greek Equivalent	Role
Jupiter	Zeus	Father, King of the Gods, Thunder, Weather, Order
Juno	Hera	Mother, Queen of the Gods, Marriage, Family
Minerva	Athena	Wisdom, War, Crafts
Apollo	Apollo	Music, Prophecy
Neptune	Poseidon	The Sea, Rivers, Earthquakes
Mars	Ares	War
Diana	Artemis	Hunting, Chastity
Ceres	Demeter	Agriculture
Venus	Aphrodite	Love, Beauty
Vesta	Hestia	Hearth, Home
Mercury	Hermes	Trade, Wealth, Travel, Communication
Vulcan	Hephaistos	Fire, Metallurgy

*Hercules was the Roman version of the Greek demigod Heracles. He travelled the world and completed 12 labors to make up for the murder of his wife and children. These trials included the killing or capture of many imposing creatures such as Cerberus, the multiheaded hound of **Pluto/Hades**.*

67

ROMAN MILITARY CULTURE

The Roman Legions

In order to survive, the Romans needed an effective army. Initially, to save costs, they had a civilian militia in which soldiers served during wartime, supplying their own weapons, and then returned to farming when finished. As they came under threat, the Romans reorganized their culture around the military. They implemented an extreme training regimen to assure discipline and adopted an honor code to never accept defeat. Soldiers were drafted at 17 years old and served for a minimum of 10 years. They organized in a legion, a unit of 5,000 men, divided into maniples of 120 infantrymen. Each maniple had different specializations to fight in different conditions. Traditional infantry had a gladius, shield, and armor. Light cavalry focused on maneuverability and quick action, while heavy cavalry with armor and chariots supplied brute force.

The Italian Wars

As their military developed, Rome absorbed the lands surrounding them. They built an alliance with the Italic peoples to their south (Latins and Samnites) to conquer the Etruscans, but they then came into conflict with their allies, conquering the Latins and then the Samnites, to control Northern Italy. This led the Greeks in Italy, led by **Pyrrhus** of **Epirus** to attack them. Pyrrhus won victory after victory, but the Romans refused defeat. This became a pattern. Rome often lost more battles than it won in wartime but outlasted its opponents and won in the decisive battles. As they conquered Italy, the Romans annexed those defeated into their military. They did not impose heavy taxes on the conquered and granted them privileges of the **Roman right**. By 265 BCE, they controlled the Italian Peninsula with an army of half a million professional soldiers.

*Each **Roman legionnaire** was trained in construction and engineering and carried equipment to build fortifications and infrastructure as needed. **Gaius Julius Caesar** stated that more battles were won by the entrenchment tool than the sword. For example, he had his men build a bridge across the Rhine in only 10 days in response to attacks from **Germanic tribes**.*

The Punic Wars

The Romans then lashed out against a new rival, the Phoenician kingdom of Carthage. The word Punic was the Latin word for Phoenicians, hence the name Punic Wars.

Carthage

Carthage became the most powerful state in the Western Mediterranean. It controlled most of North Africa and parts of Southern Europe and dominated trade in the region. They had a diverse economy, producing agriculture along the coast to go with vibrant manufacturing. Carthage had a Semitic based language and a polytheistic religion, comparable to those in the Near East at the time. As an urban, trade-based culture, they represented what the Romans opposed culturally. They nonetheless had a republican government like Rome's, with an elected legislature, balance of powers, and equivalents to consuls.

The First Punic War

Carthage and Rome came into conflict when Rome invaded Sicily. Carthage had a superior navy but had a weaker landed force. Carthage maintained an effective cavalry of horses and elephants but otherwise relied on **mercenary soldiers**. This 23-year conflict began in Carthage's favor as it ravaged Roman forces from the sea and repulsed Roman troops that landed in North Africa. The Romans invested in a navy after capturing and copying a Carthaginian ship and gradually got the upper hand. Rome conquered Sicily as its first overseas colony and forced Carthage to pay tribute. It later took Corsica and Sardinia due to a failure to pay this tribute.

The Second Punic War

Out for revenge, the Carthaginian General **Hannibal Barca** took the fight to the Romans. Hannibal led an invasion force with war elephants and 20,000 men into Europe via Spain. There, he allied with Iberian and Celtic tribes, who expanded his forces and allowed him to march through **Gaul** and attack Italy from the Alps. He raided Roman farmlands to force them to meet on his terms and regularly came out victorious. At the **Battle of Cannae**, Hannibal was outnumbered two to one but won the day by goading the

Romans to assault a choke point. Fighting for 17 years (218-202 BCE), Hannibal never lost a battle in Europe. His main problem became logistics. While Carthage was wealthy, supplies and reinforcements were hard to organize across the Alps, and Hannibal never had enough force to conquer Rome itself. In what became a **war of attrition**, the Romans refused to surrender, taking as many casualties as necessary. When General **Scipio** of the Roman forces cut off Hannibal's supply lines in Spain, the Carthaginian general retreated. Scipio took the battle to North Africa and defeated Hannibal at the **Battle of Zama** near Carthage. Scipio was given the nickname "Africanus" for his victory. The Romans then conquered the rest of the empire, sparing only the city itself.

*General Hannibal Barca gained a reputation as a great military tactician. Not only did he march his army, including elephants, across the Alps at great risk, he regularly goaded the Romans into fighting on territory of his choosing. When almost entrapped outside of **Capua**, Hannibal had his men tie torches onto cattle at night, fooling the Romans, who thought it was his army. After his defeat, Hannibal continued fighting the Romans as a mercenary general in the Near East.*

The Third Punic War, the Macedonian Wars, and Syria Campaign

A group in the Senate, led by **Marcus Porcius Cato** demanded complete conquest of Carthage to end their threat for good. The Romans invaded Carthage, destroying the city. Fearing a similar fate, the Antigonids and the Seleucids allied with Carthage to stem the Roman expansion. Despite being exhausted by the Punic Wars, Rome conquered Greece and Anatolia. Rome now had a large territorial empire, including most of the Mediterranean. A general by the name of Gnaeus Pompeius Magnus (**Pompey**) organized an invasion of Syria and the Levant.

*The **Siege of Syracuse** in 213 BCE saw a battle of wits between the great Roman strategist Marcellus and the Greek scientist Archimedes. Archimedes developed a range of defenses, including improved catapults and claws that ripped Roman ships out of the ocean. Upon Syracuse's defeat, Archimedes is said to have been killed after dismissing Roman soldiers because he was too distracted solving a geometry problem.*

The Gallic Wars

In 50 BCE, General Julius Caesar led an eight-year campaign against the Celtic tribes in Gaul, in what is now France. Caesar played the Celtic tribes off one another and formed an alliance in support of several tribes, and he forced them to submit to his authority afterwards. **Vercingetorix** unified most of the Gallic tribes to fight the Romans and initially succeeded through guerilla war tactics. At the **Battle of Alesia**, Caesar was victorious against his rival. The Roman general surrounded the city with an earthen wall, also surrounded by a moat and booby traps, along with his legions. After attempts to break free failed, Vercingetorix personally surrendered to spare his people. Nevertheless, the Romans killed indiscriminately during the war and killed over a million Celts and enslaved a million more. They instituted a campaign of destruction of the Druids. The subsequent destruction of traditional Celtic trade networks saw them decline elsewhere in Northern Europe. Where not conquered by Rome, the Celts became the victim of Germanic peoples migrating from the north.

Sculpture of Julius Caesar

Most Roman patricians had a public nickname, called a cognomen, to distinguish them from family of the same name. This name often became hereditary when the individual distinguished himself. For example, Caesar meant "the hairy," likely meant to poke fun at a lack of hair.

Changes with the Late Republic

By the first century BCE, the Roman Republic stretched from France to the Near East. Absorbing the existing cultures, the Romans reorganized their conquered territories to the political and economic needs of the Republic. While these military campaigns provided some stability, giving a common objective and keeping leaders busy, the Republic ultimately brought changes. The strain of a territorial empire caused issues within the republican government, ultimately leading to its decline.

Economics

Originally a system built upon small plot farmers, the influx of wealth from its conquests made Rome an economic behemoth. The old ideals of frugality and modesty were replaced by displays of wealth and grandeur. Less eager to expand the Latin right outside of Italy, conquest led to a mass expansion of slavery, so that by 100 CE, there were over a million slaves in Italy alone. The constant warfare sent Rome's soldier-farmers out to war, leaving slaves to do most of the work. Small farmers, either unable to compete or not wanting to return to farming after serving in the military, sold their land to wealthy elites and moved into cities. This led to a plantation system, with agriculture run by large slave gangs. Rome became an economy almost wholly dependent on slavery. Reliance on slavery reached the point where Romans would neither train nor hire free Romans for jobs, leading to increased poverty in urban areas.

Roman Slavery

While most slaves worked in agriculture, others worked in the mines or in urban areas. Jobs ranged from bookkeeping, to artisan skills, to entertainment. Slaves had a rough life. Unless skilled, slave owners had no hesitancy to work them to death, seeing them strictly as property. People were not born into slavery, but anyone could potentially be put into it as prisoners of war or through failure to pay debts. Slave revolts were regular, including one of 70,000 slaves in Sicily that defeated a Roman force before being crushed. The most famous slave revolt was led by **Spartacus**, a Thracian gladiator who recruited a slave army until he was killed. The survivors were crucified on the road to Rome to send a message.

Cultural Reactions

As Rome gained control over more foreign territories, foreign culture and ideas spread, and many Romans shifted from older traditions. Greek and Egyptian culture became popular, and wealthy Romans educated their children to be

Sculpture of Spartacus

bilingual in classical Greek and Latin. Scholars translated many foreign texts into Latin, and scholars, such as the poet **Lucretius**, promoted the Hellenistic philosophy. The Hellenistic era mystery cults became popular in Rome. This cultural influence spurred a reaction from traditionally minded Romans, such as Cato, who tried to restore traditional Roman culture. Becoming censor, Cato tried to ban Greek scholars and expelled many senators for loose morals. The statesman and orator **Cicero** later tried to split the difference, promoting the embrace of the Stoic lifestyle and Greek philosophy, but argued that happiness came with service to the state. He promoted a return to Latin as the universal language of the Republic.

Politics

As the scope of Rome expanded, new issues arose. Politicians in turn regularly feuded, leaving many issues unaddressed. Increasingly, Roman leaders turned to the general population, using populist messages or handouts to build support. Additionally, political intrigue, such as assassinations, constantly left politics in flux. One notable example was the case of the **Gracchi brothers**, Tiberius and Gaius. The Gracchi were patricians but embraced populist causes to gain leadership as tribunes. They called for reforms to cap landholding and to return to a model of small plot farming. They accused opponents of not caring about the people, while their rivals accused them of using mob rule to become dictators. Tiberius was

73

assassinated after he had the **Plebeian Council** pass a law without consulting the Senate. When his brother called for more reforms, the Senate declared him an outlaw. This type of politics became common in the Late Republic.

Rise of Generals

Increasingly, military leaders, who gained great wealth and prestige in their conquests, came to dominate Roman politics. Successful generals rose to power through support of the military and gained a popular reputation of providing order and getting things done after handing out plunder gained in conquests. An early example was **Gaius Marius** in the late 100s BCE. Marius gained notoriety after defeating the **Numidians** in North Africa. As consul, he instituted reforms to allow recruitment of soldiers from non-landowning and then non-Roman classes, while establishing an entirely professional military with soldiers paid as a full-time job. This made his troops directly loyal to him. Military leaders eventually began competing for influence. For example, when a general named **Sulla** led Roman forces into Anatolia, Marius convinced the Senate to deny Sulla's command, fearing his popularity. Sulla took command anyway and proceeded to march on Rome. Marius asserted control of the city as dictator, although he died not long after. Sulla relented after he was put in charge as dictator for three years, to stabilize the situation. He reorganized the Senate with his own loyalists, weakened the tribunes, and made requirement for holding government positions more difficult to prevent another military commander from imitating his own rise.

The Triumvirate

The First Triumvirate was an informal alliance of three politician/generals that included Caesar, Pompey, and **Marcus Licinius Crassus**, who worked together to consolidate power. The latter two gained status through military achievements. Pompey was a young commander under Sulla. An excellent

*When Julius Caesar returned to Rome, he received a **triumph** which was a ceremonial, military parade in which troops marched through Rome with their general at the rear in a golden wreath. Participants threw grain and money to the crowd, and defeated enemies were marched forward to be scorned.*

self-promoter, he gained the nickname "the great" for defeating rebels in North Africa, conquering Syria, and clearing the Mediterranean of pirates. Caesar was from an old aristocratic family and was a nephew of Marius. He had been involved in politics early in his career but had made so many enemies that he was prohibited from the city. Caesar waged the Gallic Wars, in part, to build his name by gathering military manpower, plunder, and prestige, and he wrote his **Commentaries of the Gallic Wars** to glorify himself. After serving under Sulla, Crassus became the richest man in Rome. He started his wealth by selling the land of Sulla's conquered rivals and became himself a massive landowner. He led the defeat of Spartacus. The three had been prohibited from office by the Senate due to their success and the Senate's fear of takeover. Cicero led the effort to limit their rise, devoting his life to protecting the traditional republic. With the army behind them, the Triumvirate supported each other's goals by demanding reforms in the name of the plebeians.

Caesar Victorious

When successful, the Triumvirate started competing with one another. Crassus was killed fighting against the Parthians in the Middle East, trying to expand his legacy. Caesar and Pompey then fought for power. Caesar was the more popular, due to his success in Gaul, but Pompey had the Senate name him dictator, and he declared Caesar an enemy of the Republic. Caesar refused to disband his troops, and in 49 BCE, Caesar crossed the Rubicon, the northern boundary of Roman Italy, sending the message that he would take Rome by force. Pompey fled eastward, where he had troops loyal to him, and Caesar captured Rome with minimal bloodshed. Caesar later defeated Pompey at the **Battle of Pharsalus** in Greece. Caesar followed this victory by invading Egypt, killing Ptolemy XIII, and marrying Ptolemy's sister, Cleopatra. Cleopatra became heir of Ptolemaic Egypt at 21 after leading a coup against her little brother. The two had a child named Caesarion meaning "little Caesar."

Though born in Egypt, Cleopatra's origin dated back to Macedonian Greece to Ptolemy Soter I, a general of Alexander the Great. She embraced Egyptian culture and spoke the Egyptian language. Accounts of her life included hiding in a carpet to meet Caesar and proving wealth by dissolving a pearl in vinegar and drinking it.

CHAPTER 5

The Roman Empire

THE FALL OF THE ROMAN REPUBLIC

The Beginning of the End

The rise to power of Julius Caesar marked the beginning of the end of the Roman Republic. Now an empire, Rome became less defined by the city of Rome and more by its vast territories across the Mediterranean.

The Assassination of Caesar

Julius Caesar's success in Gaul set the stage for his rise to power. Caesar's troops became so loyal to him that they supported him personally, rather than Rome itself. He was also lauded as a hero by the general population. With his position established, the Senate made him dictator for life. Caesar assumed many titles and powers, including sole right to wage war and control over government finances. He established a new 365-day calendar with a leap year called the **Julian calendar**. Fearing the end of the Republic, a group of conspirators, including **Lucius Junius Brutus** and **Cassius**, assassinated Caesar on the Senate floor on the Ides (midpoint) of March. The result was the exact outcome they had hoped to avoid.

Octavian

Mark Antony

Caesar's grand-nephew and adopted son, Octavian, was named his official heir. The people lashed out against the murder of their hero, and Octavian exploited the opportunity. Octavian formed a new triumvirate with Marcus Antonius (**Mark Antony**), Caesar's second in command in Gaul, and Lepidus, one of Caesar's longest supporters. The Senate made Octavian consul, and he organized the capture and execution of the conspirators. The new triumvirate then targeted anyone

* *

The English playwright William Shakespeare wrote several plays based on Roman history, notably his Julius Caesar. *Popular memory of Caesar's assassination often conflates the play with the historical record, notably the famous line "Et tu, Brute?" (You too, Brutus?). Caesar's last words are not actually known with any certainty.*

who had expressed opposition to its authority, notably by killing Cicero. Cleopatra fled to Egypt with Caesarion. When these purges ended, Octavian and Mark Antony started competing over influence. Antony relocated to Alexandria, where he married Cleopatra and organized to face Octavian using Egyptian resources. Mark Antony adopted Caesarian and declared him the true heir of Julius Caesar. In 31 BCE, the two faced off in the **Battle of Actium**, a naval battle north of Egypt. Octavian's forces won and proceeded to conquer Egypt and officially absorb it into the Roman Empire. Antony and Cleopatra committed suicide rather than accept capture.

IMPERIAL GOVERNMENT

Caesar Augustus

Octavian served as sole consul and gradually absorbed more powers from the other branches of Roman government. The Senate gave him the powers of proconsul but for all of Rome. In the name of the people, he was named a tribune for life, with powers to propose legislation and veto bills. As censor, he controlled taxes and oversaw written texts. He adopted the name Caesar, and the Roman emperors unofficially became known by that name until it was made a formal title 50 years later. He adopted many other titles, but most notably the epithet Augustus, or "The honorable revered one." Augustus

Sculpture of Caesar Augustus

was presented in semi-divine status as the sole guide and protector of Rome, and he required people to go to temples and perform ceremonies to honor him like a god. The emperor became the central government, and the Senate and other offices remained as little more than advisory bodies.

. . . .

Antony and Cleopatra committed suicide after their defeat by Octavian to avoid being paraded in a triumph. Cleopatra is popularly believed to have done so by having herself bitten by an asp. She likely poisoned herself by other means. Cleopatra was the last pharaoh. Rome annexed Egypt after her death and was under Roman rule.

Augustan Reforms

Augustus implemented many changes by creating a police force and fire brigade, establishing a more formalized tax system run by trained officials, and establishing an improved census. For the provinces, he let local government decurions (administrators) form councils to bring issues to him. He was a strong believer in the *mos maiorum* and organized the rebuilding and renovation of all traditional temples. He banned worship of foreign gods. Augustus required marriage and children, with fines for all unmarried men, and rewards to women with more than two children. He promoted the Latin language, exhibited by the poets **Virgil** and **Horace**, who wrote about the glories of Rome under Augustus.

While expanding the empire, he had landless Romans relocated into conquered territories as farmers. This alleviated Roman poverty and contributed to cultural integration of subject peoples into the empire.

Virgil was one of Rome's most prominent poets, notably for **The Aeneid***, which outlined the early history and founding of Rome. The Italian poet Dante, in his* **Divine Comedy***, chose Virgil as the author's guide through hell.*

Roman Emperors

Octavian died in 14 CE after turning his role as emperor into a hereditary position. The Augustan lineage became known as the **Julio-Claudian dynasty**. When emperors lacked a direct heir, they chose a designated successor. This happened commonly, as Augustus' rule passed to his adopted stepson, Tiberius. Later Caesars started choosing non-relatives, instead designating a successor and preparing him for the job. The main priority was to choose someone accepted by the Senate and military. Problems arose when an emperor failed to establish a clear lineage, which led to changes in familial dynasties over time. The early emperors included several capable administrators, such as Tiberius and Claudius, who maintained stability

Julius Caesar did not recognize Caesarion, officially Ptolemy XV, as his child because Cleopatra was not a Roman citizen. Caesar named Octavian his heir after Octavian impressed him by surviving a shipwreck while on his way to join his uncle's military campaigns. Octavian later had Caesarion executed.

and expanded territorially. Others were violent and abusive of their power, such as **Caligula** and **Nero**. In its early period, even the effective rulers were violent, and the incompetent emperors did not ruin the empire, since they were reliant on an increasingly large bureaucracy that managed the empire's day-to-day affairs.

The Five Good Emperors

The second century CE is seen as the period with the most capable emperors, as part of the **Nerva-Antonine dynasty**, including Nerva, **Trajan**, **Hadrian**, **Antoninus Pius**, and **Marcus Aurelius**. This era was the peak of the Roman Empire, with territorial expansion, internal peace, and major building projects. For example, Hadrian adopted the policy of visiting all parts of the empire, and Antoninius ruled in a period with no internal revolts. Marcus Aurelius was notable for being a "philosopher king" by being erudite and writing his own book on governing philosophy. Notable Roman monuments, such as the **Pantheon**, were commissioned and built during this period. All five embraced the practice of choosing an adopted son from an elite family and offering them training, until Marcus Aurelius chose to allow his own son to succeed him as emperor.

The Pantheon, a monument to the Roman gods, was started under Augustus but not finished in its present form until the rule of Hadrian due to damage from earthquakes. Its roof includes a perfect dome with an uncovered oculus. It remains one of the best-preserved Roman monuments, a testament to its design. It has since been rechristened as a church.

MAGRIPPA·LF·COS·TERTIVM·FECIT

Early Roman Emperors

Julio-Claudian Dynasty (27 BCE - 68 CE)
Augustus
Tiberius
Caligula
Claudius
Nero
Year of the Four Emperors (68 - 69 CE)
Galba
Otho
Vitellius
Vespasian - First of the Flavian dynasty
Flavian dynasty (69 - 96 CE)
Vespasian
Titus
Domitian
Nerva-Antonine dynasty (96 - 192 CE)
Nerva
Trajan
Hadrian
Antoninus Pius
Lucius Verus
Marcus Aurelius
Commodus

There are many accounts of Roman emperors behaving badly. Caligula is accounted as having committed violence indiscriminately, before he was killed by his own bodyguards. When a fire destroyed much of Rome in 64 CE, Nero blamed Christians and had them burned at the stake. Many accused Nero of setting the fire to justify building a new palace, and he was popularly believed to have casually played his fiddle as the city burned. Nero later committed suicide after fleeing Rome due to an internal revolt.

Roman Law

The Romans implemented a complex legal system designed to be the regulator of everyday life that was based on the principles of justice, reason, and equality. Praetors provided oversight of the legal code by defining and interpreting laws. Roman law was categorized in three parts: civil law, law of nations, and natural law. Civil law covered legal structures and applied only to citizens. The law of nations covered institutions, such as commerce and slavery, and it applied to citizens and non-citizens alike. It established clear legal contracts for relationships and ranged from business to marriage. While the first two types of law had equal weight, natural law consisted of principles that superseded man-made law and could not be infringed upon, even by a Caesar.

The Pax Romana

The early empire became identified as the *Pax Romana* (Roman Peace), as civil wars were sparse, and Rome faced little outside threat for 250 years. Augustus made a peace treaty with the Parthians and put other areas under client kings, such as **Herod** in Judaea. Military conquests continued. Under Augustus, Rome expanded northward to the Danube and Rhine Rivers, stopping there after a defeat in **Germania** at the **Battle of Teutoburg Forest** in 9 CE. At this battle, Germanic troops led by **Arminius** ambushed and wiped out three Roman legions. When the Romans invaded and conquered Britain under Claudius, the Celtic Queen **Boudicca** organized a revolt in 60 CE. Eventually Celts from across Britain joined forces and raided cities until the Romans defeated them. The Romans built **Hadrian's Wall** to guard from Celtic attacks from the north. Dacia had been an independent kingdom in what is now Romania, holding out against the Celts and Greeks. Under the leadership of King **Decebalus**, they had defeated an attempted Roman invasion. Under Trajan in the early 100s CE, Rome conquered Dacia for good to capture gold mines there. At its territorial peak under Trajan, Rome controlled the entire Mediterranean, much of Europe, the Black Sea, and the Near East. It had 26 provinces and a population of 60 million people.

*Roman meals included a condiment called **garum**, a fermented fish sauce that the Romans spread on many dishes. Yum?*

ROMAN CULTURE

Cultural Development

With the development of the empire, Roman culture increasingly became less about Rome itself as it blended with its many conquered peoples. While many Roman traditions spread to other cultures, key components of early Roman culture faded.

Military and Citizenship

Increasingly, while the army was still a regular part of Roman life, it became less central to everyday Roman identity. During the Pax Romana, Caesars used troops for labor projects instead of conquest, and increasingly the military was filled with non-Romans, as those in Italy turned to other pursuits. In the conquered provinces, the empire moved away from exclusive status for Romans and embraced a policy of assimilation. Property owners outside of Italy were allowed citizenship, as were those who served in the military. Soldiers were granted land in the provinces and were encouraged to marry local women where they settled. It was common for soldiers in any one part of the empire to end up settling in another. Cultural norms, such as clothing and food, spread between different regions, and Rome absorbed foreign gods into the pantheon. Over time, this created a cultural blending where many within the empire identified as Romans in addition to their local culture.

Urban Rome

The former Roman identity as an agrarian society faded. The Roman Empire was now largely based upon urban centers, topped by Rome itself with over one million people in the area. This was the largest empire in the world at the time. Rome was now home to a mishmash of people from across the empire. Wealthy urbanites lived in large villas with gardens that separated them from the rest of the city, which was stacked with apartment buildings. The cobblestone streets were littered with vendors who sold food and other products. Other cities in the empire followed the model of Rome in structure and facilities.

Colosseum in Rome, Italy

Entertainment

With so many people, entertainment was a necessity. This was achieved primarily with large open-air amphitheaters for plays, dances, chariot races (called circuses), or gladiatorial contests. Gladiator combat was held in huge theaters such as the **Colosseum**, built under Emperor Vespasian. In the Colosseum, they pitted fighters from different regions, organized exotic animal hunts, had public executions, and reenacted battles.

Literature and the Arts

Literature was prevalent, ranging from Virgil's account of Aeneas's life, to Horace's poems of love and **Ovid**'s reflections on mythology. Over time,

The Roman Colosseum, commissioned by Vespasian in 72 CE, was the largest amphitheater of its time and able to fit up to 80,000 people. It could even be filled with water to reenact naval combat.

literature became a protest mechanism. For instance, **Petronius** exposed Roman immorality, and historian **Tacitus** criticized the government for abandoning republicanism. Artwork spread from across the empire. Embracing Greek style realism, Roman sculptors excelled at portraits and copied classical Greek works. Of the various art forms, **mosaics** were the most unique. This art form used tiny rocks and glass to create murals and artwork. The Romans prized vibrant colors in art.

Science and Engineering

The Romans did not prioritize science in the same way as the Greeks, but the empire saw scholars such as **Pliny the Elder**, who wrote on natural history, **Galen**, who wrote on anatomy while serving as a doctor for gladiators, and **Ptolemy**, who created a map of the Earth and the most comprehensive star catalog up to that point. Roman scientific contributions in areas of architecture and engineering were mostly practical. The Romans built an elaborate road system to facilitate travel between cities and countryside. Their **aqueducts** transferred water across the empire for irrigation and supplied water to urban dwellers. This allowed Romans a relatively high level of hygiene. They invented concrete, made of lime, volcanic ash, and pumice, and this allowed sturdy items to be molded and very water resistant.

Social Organization

Rome ran on a **patronage system**. This was a hierarchical system with defined social roles and obligations for people. Wealthy elites in communities provided needs or favors to people under their patronage, such as legal services and protection. In return, these clients became beholden to their patron, working for them and showing complete loyalty. This system existed in addition to the elites' many slaves. The wealthy were also expected to contribute to the communities through public charity by

*The poet **Juvenal** wrote a collection of satirical poems and equated Roman treatment of the general population as the "bread and circuses." Under this dim view of the masses, the government kept people happy and pliant simply by providing basic sustenance and entertainment.*

building libraries, bathhouses, and theaters. For example, most aqueducts were paid for by the wealthy elites in a city. They benefited from prime access to the water supply for things such as personal bathrooms, but in turn this provided clean water to the rest of the city. A patron not living up to his obligations could be punished legally. This system had a clear power dynamic, but it built bonds among people and kept peace between them on a grassroots level. The emperor served as the patron of all of Rome.

Education

The Romans prioritized education. All children learned history, law, and military sciences, while girls learned spinning yarn and other household tasks. Mothers were responsible for teaching religion and ethics, while fathers taught business and public life. At its peak, Rome established education for all citizens, with grammar schools for ages 12-16 that taught grammar and literature and rhetoric schools for ages 16 and above that taught public speaking.

Economy

With a vibrant trade economy, each region of the empire specialized in different products. The plantation system produced mass quantities of crops (wheat, olives, grapes, cattle and sheep, etc.) that were shipped into urban marketplaces. A common currency facilitated this trade, and Rome mined massive amounts of metals (copper, tin, silver, and gold) to create the largest coinage system in the world at the time. By the 200s CE, Rome and Italy were the symbolic capital, but most economic wealth and resources were focused elsewhere, particularly in the Near East. Internationally, Roman trade reached India.

Pompeii *was a coastal port city in south-ern Italy near present-day Naples. It was destroyed in 79 CE due to the eruption of the nearby volcano, Mount Vesuvius. The city was completely covered in ash, preserving its final day into the present. These remains provide archaeologists and historians a unique, and otherwise unavailable, snapshot of Roman life at the time.*

THE STRAINS OF EMPIRE

Imperial Decline

Rome eventually stretched past its limits. Costs of managing a far-flung empire, protecting diverse borders, and paying for urban development were increasingly difficult for the central government to support financially. The empire faced military shortages with not enough troops to cover the entire border. Accordingly, designs on further expansion were stymied.

Barbarians

This was a term used by the Romans to describe the variety of peoples outside of the empire. The British Isles featured the last of the Celtic culture in Ireland, Scotland, Wales, and Cornwall. These Celtic tribes, such as the **Picts**, regularly battled the Romans while also trading with them. In the Middle East, the Parthians, a semi-nomadic tribal people from Central Asia, held the territory from Mesopotamia to the Indus River. They were expert equestrians and highly accurate using bows on horseback, a skill to which slow-moving, disciplined Roman troops were vulnerable. In Northern Europe, a variety of tribes lived in what the Romans called Germania. Exploiting the Roman destruction of the Celts, Germanic tribes conquered and settled into Central Europe. The Romans hoped to conquer the Germans but struggled in this goal due to a lack of urban infrastructure needed by the Romans to maintain their military and political system. As the Germans had no means to dislodge the empire, a status quo developed. Despite regular warfare between the Romans and Germans, and between competing Germanic tribes, they maintained an economic and cultural relationship.

Civil War

Internal factors eventually caused the Roman Empire to disintegrate from within. Leaders with no attachment to the Rome of old increasingly took charge and changed administration, while internal conflict rose. The

· ·

*The term **barbarian** originated with the Greek word* bárbaros, *and it was used to refer to all people who did not speak Greek. It meant "babbler."*

position of emperor became overtaken by generals who took power based on wartime outcomes. For example, General Septimius Severus took power after a brief civil war following Commodus, a poor leader killed by his own troops. Originally of Phoenician background from Libya, Severus avoided Rome itself and spent time with his troops before he died in England fighting the Picts. Roman soldiers became more interested in economic benefits than Roman ideology and were increasingly unwilling to participate in long, far-off campaigns. They often pledged loyalty to their local commanders rather than Rome itself. A series of assassinations lead to a 50-year period of civil war called the **Crisis of the Third Century**. Leaders in different regions claimed to be the new Caesar, with up to 26 "barracks emperors" supported by parts of the army claiming the mantle.

The destruction of trade and crop production, exacerbated by plagues, decimated densely populated urban areas. In turn, Germanic tribes such as the **Franks**, **Alamani**, and **Goths** led assaults into the empire. Several emperors were killed in battle, and many of the provinces in the Middle East were lost.

*While Rome saw much military success and territorial expansion under Augustus, it suffered a notable defeat at the Battle of Teutoburg Forest. There, an alliance of German tribes led by **Arminius** ambushed and destroyed three Roman legions. Because of this defeat, Augustus decided that formal conquest north of the Rhine was unnecessary, and it became the functional northern border of the empire.*

Diocletian Reforms

The end of civil war saw the rise to power of **Diocletian** in 284 CE. He realized that the empire was too large to manage effectively and divided administration into eastern and western halves. He claimed leadership over the wealthier east and put a friendly general, Maximian, as co-emperor in the west. These two "Augusti" each had a "Caesar" working underneath them as designated successors who managed a portion of the empire. This system divided management into four parts, known as the **tetrarchy**. Other Diocletian reforms included separation of the military and civilian leaders, the emperors excepted, and an attempted government managed economy. The Senate was no longer allowed even to give advice. Diocletian then downgraded the city of Rome to a regular province.

CHAPTER 6

Late Antiquity

MONOTHEISM IN THE ROMAN EMPIRE

Religious Shifts

From its founding, the Roman Empire maintained the Roman religion but saw challenges from monotheistic religions. Some Jewish populations resisted Roman rule as a minority population. Additionally, Christianity arose in the first century CE to grow from a minority in the empire to its most populous religion as the Roman religion faded.

The Jewish under Rome

The Romans conquered the Near East and with it a significant Jewish minority. Most of the Jewish peoples continued their traditional faith, and Rome initially allowed them to practice with few restrictions. The Romans appointed a client king, **Herod I** to rule Judaea, and a sect called the **Sadducees** ran the Temple and government administration. They promoted a strict reading of the Hebrew Bible and discouraged many supernatural beliefs. They were more open to accommodation to Hellenistic and Roman customs and rule. They were challenged by a group called the **Pharisees**, who travelled and preached reforms. The Pharisees wanted a broader interpretation of Jewish law that included oral traditions and believed in more supernatural concepts, such as spirits and angels. The Sadducees and Pharisees were two of several Jewish sects from the period that divided the faith. By the first century CE, Roman religious persecution increased, and Jerusalem became a hotbed of revolt. One such revolt in 70 CE saw the Romans destroy the Second Temple. In 135 CE, a second revolt led the Romans to destroy the city and prohibit Jewish access to it.

*The **Dead Sea Scrolls** discovered in desert caves in Israel contain some of the oldest preserved texts of the Old Testament and other documents from the first century AD. Collected there by a Jewish sect called the Essenes, they provide accounts of what life and faith was like at the time.*

Rabbinic Judaism

One notable result was that the Jewish people turned to local synagogues for worship. The **Rabbi**, Jewish teachers and mediators of Jewish law, gained prominence and likewise codified the Talmud, which outlines Jewish law in a single text. Based on the practices of the Pharisees, this movement started in Persia, where most who fled Rome relocated. This development set the stage for modern-day Judaism.

Jesus and the Founding of Christianity

Christianity arose from Judaism through Jesus of Nazareth. Born in **Galilee**, Jesus was regarded by Christians as the son of God sent to guide humanity to its salvation. Jesus was born by **Mary** via a virgin birth. She was married to **Joseph**, a distant relative of King David. The exact date of Jesus' birth is not known but was likely between 4 BCE and 4 CE and is celebrated at **Christmas**. Jesus called for reforms to purify the Hebrew faith and argued that leaders ignored the people and pursued rituals that lacked any meaning, other than making people beholden. He proclaimed that individuals had equal opportunity to be "saved" and go to heaven, should they show good behavior and charity. While he preached and performed throughout Galilee and Judaea, Jesus gained followers, such as his original **12 apostles**.

*The Temple in Jerusalem has not been rebuilt since its destruction by the Romans in 70 CE. Its only remains are the **Temple Mount** and the **Western Wall** in modern-day Jerusalem.*

The Passion

In the 30s CE, Jesus visited Jerusalem during the holiday of Passover to criticize the use of the holiday for moneymaking. Jewish leaders arrested him, condemned him of blasphemy, and turned him over to Roman authorities. The Roman governor **Pontius Pilate** made the decision to execute him based on rumors that he was trying to organize a rebellion. Resurrected two days later, Jesus set his followers on their future tasks before ascending to heaven. His death and resurrection were a new covenant established to absolve all mankind for its sins, not just Hebrews. Christianity thus formed as a new faith, with adherents trying to live out the teachings of Jesus. The Passion is celebrated on the holiday of **Easter**.

Early Missionaries

Christian missionaries spread the faith throughout the Middle East, North Africa, and Europe, led by Jesus' initial converts called apostles. Christianity appealed to different cultures by defining all individuals as equal in the eyes of God, despite previous culture and social status. **Paul of Tarsus** was particularly critical in the spread of Christianity. A former critic and persecutor of Jesus, he was reached by the Holy Spirit while travelling to Damascus. He evangelized via the Greek language and spread the faith to the **Gentiles** which were non-Hebrew Christians. Efforts made to convert the broader Jewish population were largely unsuccessful. As before, Jewish populations maintained their own faith, and the Jewish diaspora in Europe and elsewhere survives into the present. Gentiles eventually overtook Hebrews within the faith.

The Christian Bible

In the half-century after Jesus' death and resurrection, several apostles wrote accounts of Jesus' life and teachings, collectively becoming the New

*The books of the **New Testament** were written in the century following Jesus' life, largely based on the oral traditions of the time and personal accounts of the writers. Accordingly, while it serves as a holy text, it is also a work of history about Jesus's life.*

Testament. These writings, paired with the Jewish Bible, became the New Testament and Old Testament of the Christian Bible, respectively. Jesus preached in Hebrew and Aramaic, but Paul and others, such as the writers of the **Gospels**, Matthew, Mark, Luke, and John, wrote the New Testament in Greek, the lingua franca of the age.

Early Christian Communities

Christianity had most of its early success among urban populations across the Roman Empire, where missionaries were able to reach the most people. While the concept of a larger church of all Christians existed, functionally, people organized through local communities. Early Christianity spread among communities with different languages and culture, with few official doctrines other than oral accounts of Jesus' life and the teachings and writings of apostles. Everyday practices were not universally agreed upon. For example, clergy were locally organized in different structures. Some communities had bishops, originally with direct lineage from apostles, while others had just priests, preachers, or deacons, and others had no formal clergy. Some branches accepted women in clergy, but others did not.

Christianity in Europe

Although originating in the Middle East, Europe ultimately became the center of Christian civilization. This was not immediate. Although notable apostles, such as **Peter** and Paul, preached in Greece and Italy, by the 200s AD, only ten percent of Greek-speaking populations were Christian and five percent of people in Western Europe.

Sculpture of Apostle Peter

The Apostle Peter is accredited as the first bishop of Rome and accordingly the first pope in the Roman Catholic tradition. His brother, the Apostle Andrew is similarly accredited as the first patriarch of Constantinople, and thus, the first patriarch of the Eastern Orthodox Church.

Martyrdom

Roman authorities did not like the new faith and regularly tried to stamp out Christian practice wherever it grew in population and established a public presence. The Emperor Decius attempted to target Christians following a smallpox epidemic, demanding loyalty oaths to the Roman gods. Diocletian later stripped all monotheists of citizenship. Christians, believing they would move on to a better afterlife in heaven, followed the example of Jesus and accepted persecution. The concept of the Christian martyr was a central component of the early faith, and their willingness to die for their faith helped spread its popularity. Paul, for example, was arrested for "plotting revolt." As a Roman citizen, he appealed for a trial and was transferred to Rome. He preached there and won converts before he was executed.

Neoplatonism

Christianity received a boost in Roman Europe through a philosophical trend known as the Neoplatonic movement. Neoplatonism was established by Plotinus and gained popularity among wealthy Romans in the third century CE. Based on Plato's teachings, it asserted that a single supreme being had created the universe. The physical world was matter, but there was a spiritual world created from divine residue. One's goal in life was to merge the physical and spiritual world through **aestheticism**, giving up earthly pleasures to be guided by the soul. Neoplatonists became allies with Christians and blended into Christianity over time. Elements of the philosophy accordingly blended into Christian practice. For example, chastity, giving up earthly desires, gradually replaced martyrdom as the common means of making a sacrifice to Christ. Another result was a growing acceptance of Christians to recognized non-Christian teachings and practices encouraging conversion. This result is exemplified in many Christian holidays maintaining pagan traditions, as redefined to Christian terms.

*Two examples of martyrs were **Perpetua** and **Felicity**. Christians from Carthage in the third century CE, Perpetua was a wealthy noblewoman and Felicity, a slave, both mothers to young children when executed due to their faith. Perpetua's diary provides one of the oldest accounts of early Christian life and the role of women in the faith.*

ROMAN CHRISTIANITY

Constantine

The politics and religion of the Roman Empire changed drastically due to the Emperor Constantine. In the late 200s, Diocletian retired, which resulted in a new civil war called the **Wars of the Tetrarchy**. Constantine came out victorious by waiting patiently and invading Italy at the opportune time. Before the **Battle of Milvan Bridge** in 312 CE, Constantine had a vision or dream where he saw the sun overlain with a cross image. Constantine had his soldiers paint a cross on their shields and won the battle. He consolidated a single rule over the entire empire again and established a hereditary dynasty. Upon taking power, he embraced Christianity, legalizing its practice with the **Edict of Milan** in 313 CE, and began providing Christian communities state funding to help build churches. Constantine commissioned the largest basilica in the empire, **St. Peter's Basilica** in Rome.

Sculpture of Constantine

Constantinople

Constantine founded the city of Constantinople to serve as the "Second Rome," built on the Greek city of Byzantium in the Dardanelles. A hub of trade between the Middle East and Europe, Constantinople was one of the wealthiest cities in the empire. Constantine also intended Constantinople to be the new center of Christianity, given its closer proximity to the Holy Land. By this point, Rome was a second-rate city in its own empire.

*The attempt to unify the Church practices at the **Council of Nicaea** was not wholly successful. Several denominations did not accept the reforms and these included the non-trinitarian branches such as the Arians in the Germanic tribes. Most of the large, modern-day denominations splintered from the Church in later history.*

Roman Christianity

As Christians followed their emperor, Christianity went from a persecuted minority in the Roman Empire to the fastest-growing faith in the world. This process began with a formal organization, in which major cities had a bishop covering a range of the countryside around it, called a diocese. Metropolitans/archbishops led provinces, while patriarchs led the most important regions, including Rome, Constantinople, Alexandria, Antioch, and Jerusalem. Functionally, the emperor was intended to be head of the Church.

The Council of Nicaea

Given Christianity's diverse practices across communities, Constantine looked to establish a more unified and centrally run Church. In 325 CE, Constantine called the first worldwide meeting of bishops at Nicaea in Anatolia to form a common creed and universal practices. Among the many doctrines made official, the council codified the concept of the **Holy Trinity**, recognizing the Father, Son, and the Holy Spirit as the facets of God represented by Jesus. The council also decided important matters, such as which texts would be formally included in the Christian Bible. These become known as the **canonical books**. It set Sunday, the day of resurrection, as the **Sabbath** day instead of the Hebrew Saturday, God's day of rest when creating Earth. Not all embraced this consolidation, such as the **non-trinitarian denominations**, but it would become the modern organization of mainline Christianity.

Arch of Constantine in Rome

We do not know the precise dates of the watershed moments in Jesus' life, as these were not recorded at the time. The dates of major Christian holidays were set later during the reign of Constantine as days to honor these events. Easter is scheduled based on the Jewish holiday of Passover, the period when Jesus was executed. Because Passover is celebrated on a lunar calendar, both it and Easter fall on a different day each year.

Roman Churches

In Rome, individual churches took the form of basilicas, large open hallways that could fit upwards of 1,000 people. At the front, the altar was in a semicircular recess under a dome that represented the gateway to heaven. On the eastern end was the chancel or *cathedra* (throne) where the bishop sat and preached. The altar was cut off by a screen, except to clergy and choir, while the worshipers listened from the other side. The outside of basilicas featured open courtyards for social functions. Churches provided worship service, but also became centers of charity, and Constantine granted them permission to serve as small-claims courts.

Christian Theologians

The process of establishing official doctrines for Christianity occurred largely due to the work of important theologians. **Jerome**, for example, translated the Bible from Greek and Hebrew into common Latin. He also established the reading of parts of the Bible as symbolic or illustrative rather than literal. **Ambrose** promoted the idea that secular rule was subservient to God, forcing **Theodosius** to atone for his sins after Roman troops killed civilians during a revolt in Thessalonica. He also established the idea that God had a divine grace that reached people on Earth, dependent on one's purity of faith. **Augustine** wrote over 100 texts on many topics. For example, he argued that humans had received "free will" from God, and everyone had to choose whether to embrace God or submit to sin. He argued that evil entered the world because humans chose it, and God sent Jesus to show people they could still redeem themselves. These scholars also maintained pre-Christian, classical philosophies from the Greeks and Romans that fit with Christian principles. The scholar **Boethius** focused his life on this objective and brought the teachings of Aristotle into the Christian tradition. Aristotle's virtues included temperance, prudence, courage, and justice. These joined with those of the Christians, including faith, hope, and charity.

*Jesus was most likely born in the spring, not in winter. December 25 was likely chosen as Christmas, due to its proximity to the winter solstice, which was the darkest day of the year on the Roman Calendar. This reflects a symbolism of Jesus bringing light to the world. It also superseded and absorbed a major Roman holiday, **Saturnalia**, which took place on the solstice.*

Pagans

As Christianity became the largest faith in the Roman Empire, people who had not yet converted became known as pagans, a Latin word meaning "those who live in countryside." The word originally referenced Romans slow to give up the old faith and embrace the predominantly urban Christianity. It became a catchall label for all polytheistic faiths, such as the Roman and Greek religions. Constantine allowed the polytheistic religions to continue practice, as many political leaders remained firm to the old Roman religion. Nevertheless, he diverted funds from their temples. Theodosius I later made Christianity the official religion of the empire in 380 CE, banned Roman paganism, and removed pagan symbols from governmental areas. Christians tore down pagan religious monuments or had them converted into churches, including the **Pantheon** in Rome.

Northern Missionaries

St. Patrick

Consolidated in Rome, Christian missionaries proceeded to spread the faith to people in Northern Europe. The peoples in Northern Europe spoke languages far different from Latin, with polytheistic belief systems different from Southern Europe. For example, the Roman Briton **Patrick** evangelized and spread Christianity among the Celts in Ireland in the 400s CE after being held prisoner there. The Church and missionaries adapted Christianity to local customs to ease conversions. In storytelling, Christian saints took the place of old gods, attached to modified stories with a lesson to be learned from their activities. St. Patrick, for example, became a character in stories updated from earlier Celtic folklore, having him fight off the magic of Druids and pagan beasts.

*Christians later used holidays to ease conversion by absorbing pagan traditions. For example, the absorption of the Germanic holiday of **Yule**, celebrated on the winter solstice, resulted in traditions such as Christmas trees. **St. Nicholas** was the bishop of Myra in western Turkey in the late 200s CE. The stories of him merged into Yule stories about the Germanic god **Odin**. St. Nicholas accordingly evolved into the modern Santa Claus.*

THE FALL OF THE WESTERN ROMAN EMPIRE

The Decline of Rome

By the fourth century, Rome was amid a gradual decline that saw the end of the classical empire. The primary cause of this decline is widely debated, although there is no single cause. The internal pressures of maintaining a vast empire continued to weaken centralized authority, as did internal and external conflict, until parts of the empire separated into smaller kingdoms.

Administrative Division

Repeating the trend of the third century, a reunified imperial administration proved short-lived. Constantine's decision to divide the empire between his three sons led to another civil war until his second son, Constantius II, came out victorious. After a series of emperors, Theodosius I divided the empire again into two administrative halves in 393 CE. He named his sons dual emperors, one of eastern Rome and the other western Rome, with separate governing administrations. Theodosius I was the last ruler of a united Rome.

Roman Identity

Increasingly, people in the empire started to identify less as Romans and more with their local regions. Senator became a title that could be bought and was nothing more than a symbol of aristocracy. Regional leaders increasingly pushed for official autonomy within the empire. When the central government passed laws they did not like, they often ignored them with no consequences. Internal revolts became a norm, including regular peasant revolts and secessionist movements in Britannia, Gaul, and Hispania. Suppressing these revolts cost money, and soldiers increasingly were not available to a government with many other expenses.

Eastward Shift

By the late empire, the city of Rome did not hold the same credibility. Most of the imperial wealth and administrative power shifted eastward to Constantinople. The east was economically more vibrant due to its links to major trade networks. Additionally, internal issues festered in the west as it became more isolated economically and poverty grew. In addition, troops were shifted eastward to defend against a renewed Persian Empire, the **Sassanids**. Only two Roman emperors following Constantine ever visited Rome itself.

Deurbanization

Deurbanization occurred in western Rome as most of the wealth remained in the plantations. Cities became the domain of government officials and clergy, with only the major trading hubs thriving. The plantation system shifted away from slavery toward patrons who worked the land due to debts to large landowners. These people were bound to the land until they repaid their debts, which for most of them became permanent. Slaves often shifted to this category because it saved the owner from having to supply their needs. This set the stage for **serfdom** in the Middle Ages.

The Barbarian Invasions

The area north of the empire, Germania, was filled by a variety of peoples of Germanic culture and language, divided into many tribes. Although not an urban culture on the scale of the Romans, they had advanced metalworking and agriculture. While German tribes regularly fought against Rome, they at other times traded peacefully with the Romans. By the late empire, cultural exchange was normalized, as many Germans learned Latin and some embraced Christianity. Romans embraced elements of Germanic culture, such as clothing styles. Nevertheless, the cost of defending the northern border left Western Rome all but bankrupt. In response, the emperors recruited Germans to manage the borderlands for them, and German soldiers

Barbarian Warrior

gradually took over the Roman military. For example, Theodosius' top general, **Flavius Stilicho**, was a **Vandal**. These Germanic mercenaries had less training and received less support from Rome, including fewer weapons than past legions and not as much armor. The final barbarian invasions were more damaging to the relationship with Rome. This was caused by new peoples migrating from Central Asia, and these new migrants conquered territory from the Germans, pushing them to Rome for support.

Germanic Tribes in Rome

The Goths offer an illustrative case of Roman difficulty dealing with the situation to their north. The Goths, in what is now Hungary, had formerly invaded the empire but had since maintained peace with the Romans and embraced Christianity. Under pressure from the Huns in the 300s CE, a branch of the Goths, the Visigoths, petitioned to join the empire. Emperor Valens accepted them, hoping to make them into a military force. The Roman populations, however, gave them unusable land. Feeling betrayed, the Goths lashed out. When Valens marched against them, the Gothic cavalry inflicted a stunning defeat onto the Roman troops at the **Battle of Adrianople**. The Visigoths then ransacked Greece, looting and pillaging historical cities such as Athens, before they moved into Italy and sacked Rome under the leadership of a former Gothic legionnaire named **Alaric**. The Vandals, originally from Poland, followed a similar path and moved into Spain and then North Africa. They later conquered former Carthage, making a new kingdom there, and sacked Rome in the process. Other tribes, such as the Franks and **Burgundians**, followed and settled in Northern Gaul. These became independent kingdoms within Roman administration.

Germanic Religion

The Germanic tribes maintained a common religion based on many gods who represented natural elements, such as Odin and **Thor**. Much like the other polytheistic religions of the time, these gods sometimes interacted with the human world to ensure that its peoples maintained faithfulness. Most people today are familiar with the Germanic religion through Norse mythology, although the same religion was worshipped by all the pre-Christian Germanic peoples, with regional variations.

The Hunnic Invasions

The crisis that finished the Western Empire was caused by the invasion of the Huns in the early fifth century. The Huns were a nomadic warrior people who migrated into Central Europe from Asia. Their leader, **Attila**, led a 20-year conquest of peoples in Northern and Central Europe in an attempt to form his own empire. Attila led raids into Rome and demanded massive tributes in return for not attacking them. This was money Rome could increasingly no longer pay. Although Attila is often treated as the man who ended the Roman Empire, this is not actually true. At the **Battle of Chalon** in Gaul, the Romans, Visigoths, and Franks defeated Attila, and he died a few years later. Their impact was not in conquest of Rome, but in that they exposed the internal weakness and unreliability of the western empire that had fractured from within.

Artistic Depiction of Attila the Hun

Economic Decline

Shown to be militarily cowed and financially broke, the core of the empire in the west disintegrated from within by the fifth century. Trade economies in the west broke down to the point where Italy was producing at a fraction of its former levels, and poverty abounded. People, especially skilled artisans, fled eastward, so the west experienced a population decline. Many of the wealthy elite lost their fortunes with land increasingly seized by regional lords. Many of these lords had a Germanic background. People stopped paying taxes. Only urban areas maintained some degree of wealth. The Roman elite consolidated power and maintained Roman culture as it dissipated in the countryside.

The origins of Attila are broadly unknown. As far as the historical record from the time, he simply appeared on the scene in the fourth century CE. The Huns likely migrated from Central Asia as nomadic herdsmen. They developed stirrups, which allowed them to manage horses in battle as mobile archers in a way that stymied the Germans and Romans. Attila died in 434 CE due to alcohol poisoning on his honeymoon night with a young, new bride.

Germanic Kingdoms

The Germans asserted themselves by taking control of regional military units and claiming independent territory. The western empire splintered into separate kingdoms, while absorbing Roman bureaucracies. Gaul, for example, divided between the Goths, Burgundians, and Franks. These new kingdoms made their regional Latin dialects the formal language, which evolved into the modern **Romance languages**. In 476 CE, Romulus Augustulus, the last Caesar in the west, abdicated and ceded power to a new king of Italy, **Odoacer**, an Ostrogoth soldier who had led a revolt against him. Odoacer built an alliance of Germans, Huns, and disgruntled Romans to achieve victory. While western Rome disintegrated, eastern Rome survived and evolved into what historians now call the **Byzantine Empire**.

> *The last official western Roman emperor was Romulus Augustulus, "Little Augustus" which defined him as a young boy. By this point, **Ravenna** was the capital of Western Rome, and not Rome itself. The Ostrogoth King Odoacer sent Romulus Augustulus into exile, where he disappeared form the historical record.*

INDEX

110

MEET THE AUTHOR

Michael Cude is a professor of history at Schreiner University in Kerrville, Texas, where he is also program coordinator for European Studies. He completed his doctorate in history at the University of Colorado-Boulder.

Dr. Cude is originally from Central Texas but spent time living in Europe in several countries, including Romania, England, Germany, Austria, and Slovakia. He now lives in Boerne, Texas with his wife, Simona, his son, Ian, and his dog, Betty White. He still travels regularly to Europe, leading students as part of the Global Scholars program at Schreiner or visiting family in Romania. He otherwise spends his days indulging his students in more history than they ever thought they wanted to know.